Constitutional Law in Argentina

Constitutional Law in Argentina

Third Edition

Antonio María Hernández

This book was originally published as a monograph in the International Encyclopaedia of Laws/Constitutional Law.

Founding Editor: Roger Blanpain
General Editor: Frank Hendrickx
Volume Editors: André Alen & David Haljan

Wolters Kluwer

Published by:
Kluwer Law International B.V.
PO Box 316
2400 AH Alphen aan den Rijn
The Netherlands
E-mail: international-sales@wolterskluwer.com
Website: lrus.wolterskluwer.com

Sold and distributed in North, Central and South America by:
Wolters Kluwer Legal & Regulatory U.S.
7201 McKinney Circle
Frederick, MD 21704
United States of America
Email: customer.service@wolterskluwer.com

Sold and distributed in all other countries by:
Air Business Subscriptions
Rockwood House
Haywards Heath
West Sussex
RH16 3DH
United Kingdom
Email: international-customerservice@wolterskluwer.com

Printed on acid-free paper

ISBN 978-94-035-0573-2

e-Book: ISBN 978-94-035-0582-4
web-PDF: ISBN 978-94-035-0574-9

Printed in the United Kingdom.

The Author

Antonio María Hernández is Professor of Constitutional Law and Professor of Public Provincial Law and Municipal Law at the National University of Córdoba, Argentina, and Director of the Institute of Federalism of the National Academy of Law and Social Sciences of Córdoba. He received his PhD in Law and Social Sciences from the National University of Córdoba. He is Senior Fellow of the State University of New York at Buffalo School of Law (2017) and Honorary Professor of the National University of Buenos Aires (2018). He is Honorary President of the National Association of Constitutional Law of Argentina, Member of the Directive Council of the Iberoamerican Institute of Constitutional Law and the Board of Directors of the International Association of Centers for Federal Studies. He is Former Member of the Executive Committee of the International Association of Constitutional Law. He is Member of the National Academies of Law and Social Sciences of Córdoba and of Moral and Political Sciences of Buenos Aires and of the International Academy of Comparative Law, The Hague.

He is the author and co-author of more than fifty books on constitutional law, federalism, state constitutional law and municipal law, including the following.

'Reforma Constitucional de 1994' – Work of the Member of the National Constitutional Convention Antonio María Hernández, Argentine Congress Press, Buenos Aires (1995).

'Federalismo, autonomía municipal y ciudad de Buenos Aires en la reforma constitucional de 1994', Depalma, Buenos Aires (1997).

'Derecho Municipal', Volume 1, 2ª, Depalma, Buenos Aires (1997).

'Integración y globalizacion: rol de las regiones, provincias y municipios', Depalma, Buenos Aires (2000).

'El caso Fayt y sus implicancias constitucionales', National Academy of Law and Social Sciences of Córdoba, Córdoba (2001).

'Las emergencias y el orden constitucional', 2ª. Ed., Legal Research Institute of Universidad Autónoma de Mexico and Rubinzal-Culzoni Editions, Mexico (2003).

'Derecho Municipal', General Part, ed. Universidad Nacional Autónoma de Mexico, Mexico (2003).

'Derecho Constitucional', Editorial Universidad, Buenos Aires, Prologue of Giuseppe de Vergottini, with others (2004).

'Argentina' in 'Federalismo y autonomía', Director Enric Argullol Murgadas, Ariel, Barcelona (2004).

'Argentina, Subnational Constitutional Law', *International Encyclopaedia of Laws*, General Editor Prof. Dr R. Blanpain, Constitutional Law, Kluwer Law International, Suppl. 66. (2005), in English.

'Encuesta de cultura constitucional. Argentina: una sociedad anómica', Universidad Nacional Autónoma de México, Asociación Argentina de Derecho Constitucional and IDEA Internacional, with others, Mexico (2005).

'La descentralización del poder en el estado contemporáneo', Antonio M. Hernández, Director, Asociación Argentina de Derecho Constitucional and Instituto Italiano de Cultura de Córdoba, Córdoba (2005).

'Republic of Argentina', in 'A Global Dialogue on Federalism'. Volume 3. 'Legislative, Executive and Judicial Governance in federal countries', Edited by Katy Le Roy and Cheryl Saunders, Montreal & Kingston-London-Ithaca, McGill-Queen's University Press. (2006).

'Constitutionalism in times of emergency', Antonio M. Hernández, Director, Asociación Argentina de Derecho Constitucional, Córdoba, Argentina (2007).

'Derecho Público Provincial', Antonio M. Hernández, Coordinator, Lexis Nexis, Buenos Aires (2008).

'Aspectos fiscales y económicos del federalismo argentino', Antonio M. Hernández Director, Academia Nacional de Derecho y Ciencias Sociales de Córdoba, Córdoba (2008).

'Así no va más'-'Diagnóstico y propuestas de reforma político-electoral de la Provincia de Córdoba', Comisión Consultiva de Expertos, editado por las Universidades Nacional y Católica de Córdoba, Co-author (2008c).

'Aspectos fiscales y económicos del federalismo argentino', Director and Co-author, Instituto de Federalismo de la Academia Nacional de Derecho y Ciencias Sociales de Córdoba, Córdoba, (2008d).

'Argentina, Constitutional Law', International Encyclopaedia of Laws, Kluwer Law International, Suppl. 81, (2009), Holanda, in English.

'Federalismo y constitucionalismo provincial', Abeledo Perrot, Buenos Aires, (2009).

'Aspectos históricos y políticos del federalismo argentino', Director and Co-author, Instituto de Federalismo de la Academia Nacional de Derecho y Ciencias Sociales de Córdoba, Córdoba (2009).

'Argentina, Subnational Constitutional Law', International Encyclopaedia of Laws, Kluwer Law International, Suppl. 90, (2011), in English.

'Derecho Público Provincial', 2ª. Edición, Coordinator and Co-author, Abeledo Perrot, Buenos Aires, (2011).

'El caso "Fayt"', 2ª. Edición, Abeledo Perrot, Buenos Aires, (2012).

'Derecho Constitucional', 2 Tomos, La Ley, Buenos Aires, (2012), Director and Co-author.

'Fortalezas y Debilidades Constitucionales'-'Una mirada crítica en el Bicentenario', Abeledo Perrot, Buenos Aires, (2012).

'Cumplir el programa constitucional', IML, Buenos Aires, (2012).

'Argentina, Constitutional Law', International Encyclopaedia of Laws, Kluwer Law International, 2a. edition, Supl., (2014), in English.

'Derecho Municipal Multinacional', Dirección de Teresita Rendón Huerta, Ed. Porrúa, Méjico, (2015), Author of the Chapter 'Régimen municipal argentino'.

'Segunda Encuesta de Cultura constitucional. Argentina: una sociedad anómica', Eudeba, Buenos Aires, (2016), co-author with Daniel Zovatto y Eduardo Fidanza.

'La Ciudad Autonóma de Buenos Aires y el fortalecimiento del federalismo argentino', Jusbaires, Buenos Aires, (2017).

He was Vice President of the Drafting Commission of the National Constitutional Convention (1994) and of the Drafting Commission of the Constitutional Convention of the Province of Córdoba (1987) and President of the Municipal Constitutional Convention of the City of Córdoba (1995).

He served as Member of the Legislature of the Province of Córdoba (1987–1991) and of the Federal Congress (1991–1995).

His email is hernandezantoniomaria@hotmail.com.

The Author

Table of Contents

List of Abbreviations

ACHR	American Convention on Human Rights
CSJN	Argentine Supreme Court of Justice
IACHR	Inter-American Court of Human Rights
Sec.	Section
USSCJ	United States Supreme Court of Justice

General Introduction

§1. An Outline of Argentine Constitutional History

1. The area that is now Argentina was colonized by Spain in the sixteenth century.

In the debate on 22 May 1810, in the Open Assembly of Buenos Aires, the speeches of Juan José Castelli, Genaro Villota and Juan José Paso expressed the fundamental political ideas of the May Revolution: popular sovereignty, federalism and democracy.[1]

The May Revolution had two primary aims: (1) to achieve independence from Spain and (2) to organize the country constitutionally.

The first was achieved with the declaration of independence on 9 July 1816, made by the Congress of Tucumán, although the battles against Spain would not end until nearly a decade later with the triumph of the campaigns of the liberators, José Francisco de San Martín and Simon Bolívar.

The second objective was reached in 1853, when the Constituent Convention of Santa Fe sanctioned the National Constitution, establishing a federal republic.

Before this, there had been various attempts at organization: the decrees of 1810, the constitutional projects of the Assembly of 1813,[2] the Statute of 1815, the Provisional Regulation of 1817 and the unitary constitutions of 1819 and 1826, which were rejected by the provinces.

2. The adoption of federalism[3] and a decentralized system that included the municipal regime – mentioned in section 5 of the Federal Constitution – was the result of civil wars fought between 'unitarios' and 'federales' from 1820 to 1853, who created this form of government as the only means of solving the political, economic and social conflicts of a country with a large territorial extension.[4]

---

1. *See* Levene (1941:24–36).
2. Where the federal project stood out, presented by the deputies of the Banda Oriental, following the Instructions of José de Artigas. *See* Alberto Demicheli (1971).
3. *See* Hernández (2005a, 2006a and 2008a, Cap. III).
4. The political problem was the attempt to centralize the country from Buenos Aires, which was rejected by the provinces of the interior, and the economic problem linked to this caused by the handling of customs and the free navigation of the river, which also faced both players. *See* Julio Saguir (2007).

The 'unitarios', as their name implies, advocated a unitary state and were centred in urban areas, in particular in the City of Buenos Aires. The 'federales' were supported by the masses, or 'montoneras', in the rest of the country and were led by provincial strongmen, or 'caudillos'.

The original fourteen Provinces that existed before the federal state were created between 1815 and 1834. They were Buenos Aires, Córdoba, Santa Fe, Entre Ríos, Corrientes, Mendoza, San Luis, San Juan, Santiago del Estero, La Rioja, Catamarca, Tucumán, Salta and Jujuy and they arose from the cities founded by Spanish conquerors. The Provinces had sovereignty and most of them enacted Constitutions like those of Santa Fé in 1819, Tucumán in 1820 and Córdoba in 1821.

The prior existence of the provinces, and their role in creating the federal state and conferring powers on it, is reflected still in the Preamble to the Constitution: 'We the representatives of the people of the Argentine Nation, gathered in Constituent General Assembly by the will and election of the Provinces which compose it.'[5]

Through interprovincial pacts, the original provinces established the foundations of Argentine federalism, which was adopted in the Federal Constitution in 1853, with an important amendment in 1860 after the inclusion of the Province of Buenos Aires.

The first pact was that of Pilar in 1820 between the provinces of Buenos Aires, Santa Fé and Entre Ríos, followed by the 'Quadrilateral' of 1822. Among the most important are the Federal Pact of 1831, which organized the Argentine Confederation until 1852; the Agreement of San Nicolás of 1852, which led to the sanctioning of the National Constitution in 1853; and the Pact of San José de Flores of 1859, which eased the re-entry of the province of Buenos Aires into the Argentine federation and the Constitutional Reform of 1860.

3. In the battle of Caseros in 1852, General Urquiza, governor of the province of Entre Ríos, defeated General Rosas, governor of the province of Buenos Aires – in whose hands political power had been concentrated for twenty years – which led to the Pact of San Nicolás that became the basis for the sanctioning of the National Constitution at the meeting of a Constituent Assembly. Thirteen provinces were represented, each with two representatives, but without, significantly, representation from the province of Buenos Aires, which became the beginning of its secession.

The 1853 Constitutional Convention meeting in the City of Santa Fe had as its precedent the text of the 1787 Philadelphia Constitution, although it took certain differentiating features as sustained by Juan Bautista Alberdi, the father of Argentine public law, and that had an influence on his book *Foundations and Starting Points for the Organization of the Argentine Confederation.*[6]

5. *See also* Art. 121: 'The Provinces reserve to themselves all powers not delegated to the Federal Government by this Constitution, as well as those powers expressly reserved to themselves by special pacts at the time of their incorporation.'
6. *Bases y Puntos de Partida para la Organización de la Confederación Argentina.*

Because of Alberdi's influence, the original 1853 constitutional text adopted a more centralized federation than the American one, with, for example, the substantive legislation (civil, commercial, criminal and so forth) being attributed as a legislative power to the Congress, as well as the review of the Provincial Constitutions and the impeachment of provincial governors (Article 67).

In other matters, it established the same organization as that of the American federation: a federal state that allows for the coexistence of various state and governmental orders, with an allotment of competences that grants to the Federal Government only the powers expressly or implicitly delegated, while the provinces have the residual powers, in addition to their own autonomy in institutional (constituent powers), political, financial and administrative matters (Articles 1, 5, 104, 105 and 106).

Moreover, concurring competences were established for the federation and the provinces (Article 107). The Senate was established as a federal organ par excellence, with equal representation for each province of two Senators, appointed by the relevant provincial legislative branches of government, and the same representation for the Federal Capital (Article 46, currently modified as Article 54).

The text of 1853 also established that the Federal Capital was to be the City of Buenos Aires and that the Federal Government had the authority to federally intervene in the territory of the provinces (Articles 3 and 6).

4. After the secession of the province of Buenos Aires in 1853, problems continued with the Argentine federation, until the battle of Cepeda of 1859, which General Urquiza won as head of the Argentine federation. As a consequence of this victory, the Pact of San José de Flores or the 'Union Pact' (11 November 1859) was executed, which integrated the province of Buenos Aires into the federation, amending the 1853 Federal Constitution.

The Constitutional Reform of 1860 was made through a special procedure, different from that established in the 1853 text, which makes certain Argentine constitutional scholars consider this as the exercise of an original, rather than a derived, constitutional power.

It is also important to highlight that the 1860 reform made important changes to the federation, modifying certain Articles of the 1853 text in order to establish greater decentralization of power.

5. Despite the significance of this reform, the problems between the Province and the Federal Government continued until the battle of Pavón in 1861, which General Mitre won, leading to the creation of the first de facto government in Argentine history. In 1862, the victorious commander of the Province of Buenos Aires was elected President, and the national organization was led by Buenos Aires.

The highly important matter of federal ownership of the income derived from customs, which had separated the Province of Buenos Aires from the rest of the federation because the former benefited from the massive income collected through the port of the City of Buenos Aires, was definitively settled only in the 1866 Constitutional Reform.

6. Another pending problem was the fact that, since 1862, the national authorities were provisionally based in the City of Buenos Aires because the Province did not want to give up its most important city as Federal Capital. In fact, after the Reform of 1860, Article 3 of the National Constitution declares: 'The authorities in charge of the Federal Government shall reside in the city to be declared Capital of the Republic by a special law of Congress, once settled the cession of the territory to be federalized by one or more provincial legislatures.'

In 1880, the issue of the capital reached a critical point during the presidency of Avellaneda. Federal government troops confronted the Army of the Province of Buenos Aires, under Governor Tejedor Commander-in-Chief. The blood of 3,000 soldiers sealed the capitalization of Buenos Aires, which was subsequently confirmed by Congress (Law 1029) that same year, with the agreement of the Legislature of the Province.[7]

At the end of the nineteenth century (1898), there was another constitutional reform modifying the number of ministers of the presidency and the population base for making up the national Chamber of Deputies.

7. In the first decades of the twentieth century, the principal event in constitutional policy terms was the passing of Law 8871, called the 'Sáenz Peña Law'. This law established political rights, recognizing individuals' rights to universal, equal, secret and obligatory suffrage. The political regime thus underwent a significant change, transferring power from the educated minorities that had exercised it until then to the popular majorities. And it was in 1916 that the Union Cívica Radical came to power with the election of Hipólito Irigoyen as President, the first President of Argentina to be elected democratically. This historical cycle was interrupted in 1930, with a military coup that inaugurated a period of institutional instability, which would end only in 1983.

8. The coming to power of Juan Domingo Perón in the military coup of 1943 should be noted because it gave rise to the movement that bears his name and that has had great political influence that remains to these days.

In his first constitutional government, which began in 1946, Perón promoted the Constitutional Reform of 1949, with the aim of making presidential re-election possible and incorporating the postulates of social constitutionalism into the National Constitution. However, various Provincial Constitutions anticipated this incorporation, as will be seen in paragraph 11. There had also been social and labour legislation as from the beginning of the twentieth century.

9. In 1955, there was an other coup d'état in Argentina, against Perón. A few months later, in April 1956, the de facto government took constitutional power on itself and abrogated the 1949 Constitution through a decree. In its place, it declared the Constitution of 1853 with its reforms of 1860, 1866 and 1898 to be in force. Later, the military government convoked a National Constituent Convention, declaring the need for a constitutional reform, in an autocratic exercise of pre-constituent power.

7. *See* Hernández (2008c:603–604).

The National Constituent Convention of 1957, meeting in Santa Fe, ratified the currency of the Constitution of 1853 that the de facto government had re-established, with its reforms of 1860, 1866 and 1898. It also incorporated a set of social rights into the Constitution, which are still in force today as Article 14*bis*.

In 1972, Law 19.608, dictated by a de facto government, decreed the sanction of a fundamental statute that reformed various Articles of the 1853 Constitution. This statute, which, among other changes, established double voting for presidential elections, governed the elections held in 1973, which brought in a new constitutional government until 1976. The full force of the 1853 Constitution was re-established with the return of democracy on 10 December 1983 after the last coup d'état that occurred in 1976.

10. A new National Constituent Convention met in 1994 and profoundly reformed the Constitution that is now the current text.

Law 24.309 – declaring the need for the reform – obtained the majority vote to enact reform required constitutionally by Article 30 of the Supreme Law, that is, more than two-thirds of the total members of each of the chambers. The representatives were elected in entirely clean elections, under the rule of law and of the public liberties. Regardless of the objections made to the law – overcome with the adoption of its Regulation by the Convention[8] – nowadays the debate seems to have quietened down.

The Convention, meeting in the cities of Santa Fe and Paraná, had 305 representatives – the sum of the number of members of the Congress (257 Deputies and 48 Senators at that time) – representing 19 political blocs. This Convention had the highest attendance in the history of Argentina; the delegates completed their task in only ninety days, in an exemplary context of democratic pluralism, as the different political parties agreed, producing important constitutional reform, both in its dogmatic part and in its organic part. The representatives achieved a high degree of agreement for the sanctioning of sixty-one constitutional norms: Twenty new, twenty-four reformed and seventeen transitory provisions.

In the broad context of Argentina's constitutional history, this is the reform with the greatest legality and legitimacy, and it also concluded painful periods of frustration and misunderstanding, which seriously affected the life of the nation. This Constitutional Reform was made in the longest democratic process in Argentina since 1930, and so it is perceived as the culmination of the political and legal experience, expressing the most important moment in the exercise of politics in Argentina in modern times.

11. As we have seen, various stages of constitutional law have been recognized based on the promulgation of the historic Constitution of 1853, and related to other moments of constitutional reform:

---

8. For a discussion of historical circumstances of the Regulations of the Convention, which included the question of the legality and legitimacy of the reform, *see* Quiroga Lavié (1996).

(1) liberal or classic constitutionalism, which consecrated the liberal rule of law and recognized first-generation human rights (civil and political rights), from the sanctioning of the National Constitution in 1853 to the middle of the twentieth century;
(2) social constitutionalism, incorporated into the text of the federal Magna Carta in the Reforms of 1949 and 1957, which established a social state and recognized the second-generation human rights (social rights); and
(3) the constitutionality of the internationalization of human rights, a product of the 1994 Reform, which gave constitutional hierarchy to certain international treaties on human rights and recognized the third-generation rights (right to a healthy environment, user and consumer rights, right to peace and human development).

In general, the Provincial Constitutions were adapted to these changes.

However, in the transit towards social constitutionalism, some Provincial Constitutions were ahead of the Federal Constitution, as in the case of the Provinces of Mendoza (1916), San Juan (1927), Entre Ríos (1933) and Buenos Aires (1934), which already acknowledged the social rights of workers or votes for women, while these were introduced at the federal level only in 1949 and 1957.

And in relation to the third stage, the Provincial Constitutions of Neuquén (1957), San Juan (1986) and Córdoba (1987) already included among their supplementary provisions some international treaties on human rights, in addition to acknowledging third-generation human rights, as for instance those related to the environment provided for in the 1987 Córdoba Constitution, whereas these were in the 1994 Reform of the Federal Constitution.

12. As is the case with other countries in Latin America, Argentina has experienced serious difficulties with the stability of its political system. This is evidenced, for example, by the series of military coups d'état that took place between 1930 and 1983 (in 1930, 1943, 1955, 1962, 1966 and 1976) disturbing both constitutional order and democracy. This instability has been a major cause of the centralization of power, with successive rounds of constitutional violations that impeded the exercise of provincial and municipal autonomies.

Although Argentina fortunately returned to a democratic form of government in 1983, the performance of state institutions remains, in many ways, unsatisfactory. It is clear throughout history, and especially now, that the executive branch has always exceeded in the exercise of its attributions over the legislative branch, without adequate control from the judicial branch.

As we see later, Argentine 'hyperpresidentialism' has affected the checks and balances and the federal system as well, consolidating a process of political, economic and social dependence of the provinces on the national sphere of government. This situation was aggravated by permanent states of emergency. The past twenty-five years have been marked by a lack of institutional quality, suggesting an underlying political and legal immaturity that must be overcome.[9]

9. *See* Hernández (2003a).

§2. Outline of Argentine Geography and Population

13. Geographically, Argentina is a very large country, with a continental land surface of 2.8 million square kilometres. There is substantial asymmetry in the geographical size of the provinces into which the state is divided, ranging from the province of Buenos Aires with an area of 307,571 square kilometres, to the much smaller provinces of Tucumán and Tierra del Fuego, with surface areas of 22,524 and 21,263 square kilometres, respectively. The Autonomous City of Buenos Aires is smaller still, with a land surface of only 200 square kilometres. There are substantial differences also in the distribution of the population between the constituent parts of the federation. Of a total population estimated at 44 million, approximately 16 million live in the Province of Buenos Aires, and more than 3 million people live in each of three other areas with a relatively concentrated population: namely, the provinces of Córdoba and Santa Fe and the City of Buenos Aires. By contrast, the population of the province of Tierra del Fuego is slightly more than 200,000.

14. The population of Argentina is relatively homogeneous, apart from the proportionally small number of aboriginal people[10] whose pre-existence and cultural identity are recognized in the Constitutional Reform of 1994.[11] The country received waves of immigration, mainly from Spain and Italy, at the end of the nineteenth century and at the beginning of the twentieth century. The people overwhelmingly share a common language, common religion and common culture.

10. Approximately 1% or 2%.
11. Article 75, Clause 17.

Part I. Sources of Constitutional Law

Chapter 1. The Constitution

§1. Typification

15. The Argentine Constitution belongs to the group of 'written' and 'codified' constitutions, that is, those characterized by the uniting of all their norms into a single document.

It can also be classified as 'rigid' because it can be modified only through a special procedure regulated in its Article 30, which is different from that established for the enactment of common legislation.

Nevertheless, since 1994, it also has some aspects of a 'flexible' constitution, that is, it permits amendments through the same mechanism employed for common legislation. This arises from the capacity that Article 75, Clause 22, the final part, gives the National Congress, through an aggravated majorities procedure, the authorization to give constitutional status to new treaties on human rights.

16. It is also a 'mixed' constitution because it has elements of rational normativism and of traditional historicism.[12]

The Argentine Constitution most closely resembles the first type in its original enactment in 1853 and in 1860, both in its dogmatic part with its recognition of rights and guarantees and in its organic part with the division and limitation of state powers.

However, it also has elements of traditional historicism, for example, in Article 29 which prohibits the granting of extraordinary powers or the total public authority, as occurred with the dictatorship of Juan Manuel de Rosas (1833–1852). Likewise, we could point to the confessional clauses, such as Article 2, by which the Federal Government 'supports' the Roman Catholic Apostolic religion; or the invocation of God contained in the Preamble and in Article 19, when referring to the

12. According to the typology of Manuel Garcia-Pelayo (1961), we can distinguish three types of establishment: (1) rational-normative, (2) historical-traditional and (3) sociological. The rational-normative type corresponds to the first stage of constitutionalism in the world. It is a consequence of the illuminist ideal of government of law, with constitutions of universal validity, as explained by Art. 16 of the Declaration of the Rights of Man and the Citizen of the French Revolution of 1789. However, the historical-traditional type was the response of romanticism and historicism, which came primarily from Prussia, where the idea arose of the right of peoples to their own legal structure and the traditionalist theses were preferred.

private actions of men, and also the clauses on the prohibition of internal customs, in Articles 9–12, and on free navigation of the rivers, in Article 26.

17. In its ideological content, the Argentine Constitution also has a mixed composition, reflected in the various stages that constitutionalism passed through, as we saw in the General Introduction. Thus, in the first stage, its norms reflected classic or liberal constitutionalism, recognizing civil and political rights. Later, it consecrated the principles of social constitutionalism in the Constitutional reforms of 1949 (later abandoned) and 1957. In terms of rights, this meant the recognition of the social rights that had become widespread in Europe after the Second World War. Finally, the Constitutional Reform of 1994 brought in the third stage of the internationalization of human rights, particularly in Article 75, Clause 22.

18. In terms of the influence of foreign law on Argentine constitutionalism,[13] at the federal level, the original Constitution of 1853 and 1860 was based on the model of the US Constitution of Philadelphia of 1787. In the Constitutional Reform of 1994, however, Argentina relied on the influence of European law. Thus, over a presidentialist and federal model, new institutions were accepted that found their origin in European parliamentary models. Among these new institutions are the Magistrates Council, the Impeachment Jury, the Ombudsman and the Head of the Cabinet of Ministers.

Other contributions to the Argentine Constitution are derived, finally, from the development of so-called community law, reflected in the constitutionalization of regional integration processes, as provided for in Article 75, Clause 24 also incorporated in the 1994 Constitutional Reform.

§2. Structure of the Argentine Constitution

19. The Argentine Constitution is structured as follows: a Preamble; a First Part (Articles 1–43), called dogmatic; a Second Part (Articles 44–129), called organic; and finally, seventeen Temporary Provisions.

The *Preamble* is a brief statement of the principles, values and purposes inspiring Argentine society. It contains statements on liberty, equality, peace, justice, common security and form of representation, which are useful for clarifying the interpretation of the text of the Constitution.

20. The *First Part*, termed *dogmatic*, contains the declarations, rights and guarantees. This part has two Chapters: (1) 'Declarations, Rights and Guarantees' and (2) 'New Rights and Guarantees'. The Chapters have Articles, and some articles have Clauses, and finally, some Clauses have Paragraphs.

The *declarations* are solemn statements on human beings, society and the state. Thus, section 1 declares that Argentina is organized as a nation adopting the representative, republican and federal form of government.

---

13. *See* Hernández (2005e).

The Constitution establishes a set of civil rights, proper to classical constitutionalism (Articles 14, 16, 17 and 20); political rights (Articles 37 and 38[14]); social rights (Article 14*bis*[15]); and the new rights, called third-generation, such as the right to a healthy, balanced environment, suitable for human development and productive activities or the rights of users and consumers (Articles 41 and 42[16]).

The Argentine Constitution includes generic guarantees concerning due process (Article 18) and a broad range of guarantees such as the injunction, habeas data, protection of sources of information for journalists and habeas corpus (Article 43).

In Article 75, the Constitution lists the powers of the National Congress, naming in Section 22 eleven international human rights instruments that have constitutional hierarchy, each of which in turn regulates a diverse set of rights and guarantees.

21. The *Second Part*, on 'Authorities of the Nation', refers to the organization of power and is divided into two titles: (1) 'Federal Government' and (2) 'Provincial Governments'.

The first title identifies the organization of the republican system under the principle of the separation and balance of powers: legislative, executive and judiciary, each covered in Sections, which in turn are divided into chapters.

The Legislative Power Section refers to the organization of the Congress, the structure of which is bicameral: a Chamber of Deputies represents the people of the provinces and a Senate represents the provinces. It defines the requirements and method of election of its members, their terms of office, incompatibilities and immunities, powers and their mode of operation. In addition, there is a special chapter on the mechanism for forming and enacting the laws.

The Constitution also includes control institutions, such as the ombudsman and the General Auditing Office of the nation.

Then, the Constitution prescribes the composition of the executive power in one division, with different chapters that establish the method of election, vacancy and other general conditions for the exercise of the offices of President and Vice President. Aspects related to this body, in charge of executive, political and administrative functions, are also considered. The tasks of the executive power are performed by an organic structure headed by the President, who, as political head of the general administration of the country, gives directives, instructions or regulations for its better performance.

Another Section regulates the state's judicial power, which exercises constitutional control and especially the judicial review. The judicial function is exercised exclusively by the judicial branch, the highest authority of which is the Supreme Court of Justice of the Nation. The Constitution defines its jurisdiction and competence. The guarantees of the exercise of this function are also determined. The mechanism of selection and removal of lower magistrates is also established. For this purpose, after the 1994 reform, the Council of the Magistracy and the Jury of Impeachment were established. Likewise, in the fourth Section, the Constitution incorporated the Public Ministry in the reform of 1994.

---

14. Incorporated in the Constitutional Reform of 1994.
15. *Ibid.*, 1957.
16. Also incorporated in the Constitutional Reform of 1994.

The second title is concerned with the Provincial Governments. The subnational bodies of the federation are regulated, that is, the Provinces and the Autonomous City of Buenos Aires. The Provinces enjoy autonomy and have their own institutions, elect their authorities and dictate their Constitutions. They also conserve all the powers and competences not delegated to the Federal Government through the Constitution.

The Autonomous City of Buenos Aires was created in the 1994 Constitutional Reform, with the special constitutional status of city-state, with a degree of autonomy very similar to that of the Provinces.

The Constitution also establishes the bases of the municipal organization as an obligation of the provincial states, in virtue of the provisions of Articles 5 and 123. The Provinces may only establish an 'autonomous' municipal regime, ensuring their institutional, political, administrative and economic-financial aspects. There are no intermediate local bodies in Argentina between the municipalities and the provincial states.

22. The *Temporary Provisions* are clauses that concern the problems arising from the change in constitutional norms and that, in general, expire within a certain period. They are part of the Constitution and have the same normative hierarchy.[17]

It is particularly important the first temporary clause, concerning the situation of the Malvinas (Falklands), South Georgia and South Sandwich Islands:

> The Argentine Nation ratifies its legitimate and non-prescribing sovereignty over the Malvinas, Georgias del Sur and Sandwich del Sur Islands and over the corresponding maritime and insular zones, as they are an integral part of the National territory. The recovery of said territories and the full exercise of sovereignty, respectful of the way of life of their inhabitants and according to the principles of international law, are a permanent and unrelinquished goal of the Argentine people.

§3. Procedure for Reform: Declaratory Law of the Need for Reform and Constituent Convention

23. The total or partial reform of the National Constitution is provided for in Article 30. It is realized through a two-step procedure: the so-called pre-constituent stage, which is the responsibility of the Congress, and the reform itself, which is the responsibility of a constituent convention or assembly called for the purpose.

Congress, with the vote of two-thirds of its members, must declare the need for the reform, which may be total or partial. This declaration, which normally takes the form of a law, states the points or sections for reform if this is partial and convokes a constituent convention. The laws declaring the need for constitutional reform can also set formal and material limits for the activity of the convention. For

17. Bidart Campos (2000a:338).

this, in practice the declaratory law usually determines the place or venue of the deliberations of the convention, as well as the deadline for it to complete the task of reform.

24. The reform can be made only by a 'Constituent Convention' or 'Constituent Assembly' brought together for that purpose, made up of representatives elected by the people. The make-up, eligibility requirements, incompatibilities, immunities and privileges of the representatives are set by the declaratory law.

Regarding the powers of reform that the Reforming Constitutional Convention has, it is sovereign, but within the time and material limits set by the law declaring the need for reform.

§4. THE REFORM OF 1860

25. In brief, the structure of the text promulgated in 1853 consisted of a Preamble, a dogmatic part, an organic part and Temporary Provisions.

As seen in paragraph 4, the 1860 reform brought about important changes in the federation because it modified certain sections of the 1853 text in order to establish greater decentralization of power. It is evident that this was the purpose of abrogating the rules that established the review by the Congress of the Provincial Constitutions, as well as the possibility of impeachments of provincial governors before Congress.

Additionally, it modified the wording of two important sections: (1) Article 3 about the Federal Capital and (2) Article 6 about federal intervention. In the first case, it established the same principle as Article 13, that is, of territorial integrity in the creation of new provinces, which meant that the territory of the Federal Capital had to be established by a law of Congress, with the prior assignment of the relevant territories by the legislative branch of the province or provinces involved (Article 3).

In Article 6 on federal intervention, the wording of the reasons for intervening was refined so as to reduce the free determination of the federal authorities, establishing the requirement of a prior request on the part of the provincial authorities to the Federal Government for support in case of insurrection, sedition or invasion by other Provinces.

§5. THE CONSTITUTIONAL REFORMS OF 1866, 1898, 1949, 1957, 1972 AND 1994

26. One very important issue that had separated the province of Buenos Aires from the rest of the federation was the ownership of the Federal Customs revenues. The Federal Government made use of this income, which was based on the huge amounts deriving from the port of the City of Buenos Aires.

The matter was finally resolved only in the Constitutional Reform of 1866, which amended sections 4 (giving it its current wording, referring to the formation of the national treasury) and 67, Clause 11, allowing export duties for the nation for an unlimited period.

27. The last Constitutional Reform of the nineteenth century was in 1898, modifying the number of ministers accompanying the President of the Republic and the population base for making up the National Chamber of Deputies.

These issues basically reflected the increase in population that occurred in Argentina in the last decades of the nineteenth century. This was for several reasons. First, waves of immigrants arriving in the country produced a considerable increase in the population. Second, since 1869 periodic population censuses gave a more accurate count of the number of people living in Argentina. And third, the incorporation of a vast geographical area into the territory of Argentina after the so-called Desert Campaign, consisting of the conquest of areas hitherto occupied by native peoples, increased the population.

28. The Constitutional reform of 1949 produced changes both in the organic and dogmatic parts. Presidential re-election was made possible, and the postulates of social constitutionalism were incorporated into the text of the Constitution.

Although the text[18] explicitly stated in its Preamble the 'decision to constitute a socially just, economically free and politically sovereign Nation',[19] it did not expressly accept the rule of social law, as other constitutional texts had done.[20]

Article 37[21] of this text contained the right to work and other rights, referring to the employment relationship, social security, the elderly, education and culture, health, welfare, the protection of the family, economic progress, a healthy and sufficient diet and clothing, among others.

Articles 38, 39 and 40 related to the social function of property, extended to capital and to economic activity, respectively.[22] It did not, however, contain the right to strike, which gave rise to some controversy, even among representatives belonging to the majority reform project.[23] According to Sagüés (1997), 'a new constitution was designed, inspired by an ideological conception different from the previous one, inspired by the social vision of justicialism. It is popularly known as the "Peronist constitution"'.[24]

This reform was questioned by the political opposition and by the doctrine. The validity of the process was objected to from the moment of its convoking because to declare the need for reform the National Congress did not gather the two-thirds

18. 'Constitución Justicialista', Presidencia de la Nación, Subsecretaría de Informaciones, 1949.
19. *Ibid.*, 5–6.
20. For example, the Fundamental Law of Bonn of that year and previously the Constitutions of France and Italy.
21. *Ibid.*, 32–50.
22. *Ibid.*, 51–55.
23. *See* the opinion of the convention representatives Sampay, in favour of non-inclusion, and Ramella, the opposite position, in Ekmekdjian (1993:18–19); Vanossi (1982:314–315).
24. Sagüés (1997, 1:180).

of votes of the members of each chamber but only of those present, contrary to the spirit of Article 30 of the Argentine Constitution.

In addition, various reforms were introduced that aimed at a greater concentration of power instead of its rationalization: (a) the inclusion, together with the already existing state of siege, of the 'state of alert and alarm' (Article 34)[25] that could be declared by the executive branch (Article 83, Clause 19)[26] with consequent limitations to individual rights and guarantees; (b) the extension of military jurisdiction – mitigated by the incorporation of the habeas corpus (Article 29);[27] (c) the diffuse 'cooperation requested by the Federal Government' added to the requirements for provincial autonomy (Article 5);[28] and (d) among the powers of the executive branch (Article 83, Clause 23),[29] the breadth of the declaration 'provides whatever conduces to the order and structure of public services', even though the legislation remained the responsibility of the Congress (Article 68 inc. 13).[30]

So it was no wonder that the main opposition party, the Radical Civic Union, retired from the Constituent Convention. It is clear that it was a constitutional text that had neither consensus nor sufficient agreement among the political forces and that reflected a climate of high tension and division in Argentine society.[31]

29. The 1949 Constitutional Reform was in force for only a short period because in April 1956 a decree of the de facto government, that had begun with the coup d'état of 1955, abrogated it and declared the Constitution of 1853 with its reforms of 1860, 1866 and 1898 in force.

To this autocratic exercise of constituent power was added later the calling of a National Constituent Convention declaring the necessity of constitutional reform.[32]

---

25. 'Constitucion Justicialista', Presidencia de la Nación, 29–30.
26. *Ibid.*, 98–99.
27. *Ibid.*, 23–25.
28. *Ibid.*, 9.
29. *Ibid.*, 100.
30. Among authors who have taken a critical position emphasizing the likely concentration of power, Ekmekdjian (1993:18–19) and Vanossi (1982:296) refer to the possibility that the Constitution is provided to enhance the quality controls on political parties (s. 15), the extension of the scope of criminal punishment (s. 21), and they refer to other clauses in the organic part reinforcing the concentration of powers in the hands of the executive.
31. As Nino (2005:64) remembers, 'The Justicialist experience made many think in Argentina, which has had a strong influence on the consciousness of large sectors, that social justice is incompatible with values related with respect for legality and the rule of law, with freedom of expression, tolerance of opposition, respect for the separation of powers, the clean electoral procedures, etc.' Remember that in the official government publication, this reform was named 'Justicialist constitution'.
32. The commission designated for that purpose by the Provisional Executive was composed of Drs Sebastian Soler and Juan A. Gonzalez Calderon, who claimed that the de facto government had authority to annul the 1949 Constitution and then convene a convention to ratify the decision. Given these circumstances and those surrounding the 1957 Convention, it was claimed years later that it was unconstitutional. *See* Consejo para la Consolidación de la Democracia (1986:269–275). These debates on the legality and legitimacy of the constitutional reforms undoubtedly affected the legal order. And this is why we believe that only the constituent power was able to resolve these issues, as the National Constituent Convention of 1994 did, which ended this discussion by stating that the Constitution is that of 1853 with the reforms of 1860, 1866, 1898, 1957 and 1994.

The National Constituent Convention of 1957, meeting in Santa Fe, ratified the currency of the Constitution of 1853, which the de facto government had re-established, with its reforms of 1860, 1866 and 1898.

It also incorporated a set of social rights to Articles 14*bis*[33] and 67, Clause 11 (today Article 75, Clause 12) conceding to the Federal Congress the power to dictate the Code of Labour and Social Security.

Section 14*bis* basically protects the worker it covers labour relations, collective working rights (unionism, strike and so forth) and social security. Even though the text 'takes on the most classical and traditional of individual and collective labor law' (Bidart Campos, 1999: 407–408), it should not be understood as a closed or exhaustive list.

This reform was also criticized in its handling and legitimacy because of the pre-constituent function that the de facto government gave itself, ignoring the procedure of Article 30 of the Constitution. Another criticism arose from the political proscription of the Justicialist party, which was undoubtedly the majority at that time. Finally, the convention remained without quorum and was unable to continue. In any case, the norms sanctioned were incorporated into the National Constitution and nowadays are part of the current text, ratified in 1994.

30. In 1972, Law 19.608 dictated by a de facto government, exercising autocratic constituent power, decreed the sanction of a *Fundamental Statute*, which reformed various Articles of the 1853 Constitution.

The main reforms were introduced in the organic part. Among these, the mandates of deputies and senators were unified at four years; the popular election of senators was decreed, to be three per province;[34] the period of sessions of Congress was extended; the President's re-election was enabled, shortening its mandate to four years, and establishing popular election by a two-ballot system (ballotage); and a mechanism was installed of juries for the removal of lower judges.

The statute was in force for the elections held in 1973 to consecrate the return to constitutional government. In 1976, there was the last coup d'état that dictated a new statute. Finally, the full force of the 1853 Constitution was re-established with the return of democracy on 10 December 1983.

31. The Constitutional Reform of 1994[35] was arranged in a political agreement named the 'Pact of Olivos'; it was signed at the end of 1993 by the leaders of Peronism and Radicalism Parties, Carlos Saúl Menem and Raúl Alfonsín, and was then ratified by their political forces.

This agreement included various topics that were then expanded in the *Nucleus of Basic Agreements*, written by a Commission of Jurists of both political parties and

---

33. *See* Jaureguiberry (1957).
34. In the 1853 Constitution, the mandate of senators was nine years; two were elected per province, and they were appointed by the provincial legislatures.
35. In the literature, this process has been extensively tackled. *See*, among others, the book *A 10 años de la Reforma de la constitution Nacional*, published by the Argentine Association of Constitutional Law in 2005.

that enabled the declaratory law of the need for reform (Law 24.309), which obtained more than two-thirds of the votes of all the members of Congress.[36]

To evaluate a constitutional reform, the three periods of the constituent process should be considered:[37] the 'pre-constituent', declaring the need for the reform, responsibility of Congress and culminating with the popular election of the representatives;[38] the 'constituent', with the convention, exercising the constituent power and sanctioning the reforms; and the 'post-constituent', including the regulation and compliance with the reform produced.

32. In the reforms introduced in 1994, there were six main ideas guiding the task of the Convention, which we pointed out in the foundations of our overall project of Reform of the National Constitution, presented in the Constituent Convention:[39] (1) the attenuation of presidentialism; (2) modernizing and strengthening Congress; (3) ensuring the independence of the judicial branch; (4) the strengthening of federalism and municipal autonomy; (5) the provision of a new status to the City of Buenos Aires; and (6) the recognition of new rights and constitutional guarantees.

It is worth analysing whether the design of the constituent assembly matched the main ideas guiding the reform, so this is our personal assessment of each of these.[40]

The first, the *attenuation of presidentialism*, sparked the greatest controversy, with various criticisms given to the continuation of the phenomenon of 'hyperpresidentialism'.

We think that, in general, the changes introduced in the text were correct, even though in the sociological reality they have not been complied with.

To correct the strong presidentialism, the 1994 constituent assembly adopted the following principal modifications:

(1) depriving the presidency of one of its responsibilities in the Federal Capital, in which it had historically been able to designate alone the Mayor of the City of Buenos Aires;
(2) strengthening Congress through various reforms, to be analysed later, aiming at a better balance of powers within the republican system. These included the

36. This Nucleus of Basic Agreements was then presented as a project of constitutional reform by those parties in the National Constituent Convention, which finally gave it their approval with broad consensus. We personally participated in all stages of the legislative and constitutional process, in our capacity as a member of the Commission of Jurists of the Pact of Olivos, as Vice President of the Bloc of National Radical Deputies and Vice Chair of the Drafting Committee of the Constituent Convention of 1994.
37. *See* Hernández (2005a).
38. On the first pre-constituent phase, *see* the General Introduction, para. 10 and Hernández (2005a).
39. *See* our Project of Constitutional Reform, which covered all the points of the reform as decided by the declaratory Law 24.309, presented in the National Constituent Convention of 1994, as Bill N° 72, to be found in the *Diario de Sesiones de la Convención*. *See also* Hernández (1995a:26) and the Appendix in Hernández (1997a).
40. For a more detailed analysis, *see* Hernández (2005a).

extension of the ordinary period of sessions, greater powers for the declaration of federal intervention, the creation of the position of Chief of the Ministerial Cabinet who must make a monthly report to each House and may be removed by a vote of censure and the creation of monitoring bodies that are functionally related to it;

(3) reducing the powers of the President in appointing the members of the judicial branch through the creation of the Council of the Magistracy and the procedure established for the ministers of the Supreme Court;

(4) strengthening provincial and municipal autonomy to reduce the powers of the Federal Government and to assert the vertical control of power as another objective of federalism;

(5) giving constitutional status to supervisory bodies like the General Auditing Office of the nation, the Ombudsman and the Public Ministry, aiming to deepen the control proper to the republican system;

(6) reducing the President's mandate to four years, with a possibility of immediate re-election and direct election, as had been demanded for years by most political parties, the constitutional doctrine and precedents of 1949, 1957 and 1972, as well being the dominant trend in comparative law, including that of Latin America;

(7) incorporating in the Constitution decrees of necessity and urgency and delegated legislation, as emergency institutes validated by the case law of the Supreme Court from the *Peralta* (1990) and *Delfino* (1927) cases and with the indisputable purpose of limiting the powers of the executive branch in their exercise, as emerges from the Article 99, Clause 3 and Article 76 and the debates of the Constituent Convention; and

(8) creating the chief of Ministerial Cabinet, as a rather hybrid institution being of parliamentary origin in a presidential system and with the aim of moderating hyperpresidentialism and serving to ensure governability in situations of political crises, as is also shown in the constitutional letter and the debates.

Although we agree with the normative design made by the convention, we believe that because of lack of compliance with the Constitution and continuous violation of the law, no attenuation of hyperpresidentialism has been seen as the constituent assembly legislated. Although the partial limitations listed in points 1, 3, 4 and 5 functioned effectively, there is no sign that the other points have achieved their purpose. In particular, we would criticize the Congress's abandonment of its powers, the excessive use of decrees of necessity and urgency and of legislation delegated by the President, and the institutional practice of the Chief of Ministerial Cabinet, which has in no way diminished the presidential powers or served so far in a crisis situation, such as that at the end of 2001 during the presidency of De la Rua.

Of the norms drawn up, Article 76 on legislative delegation deserves special mention for its brevity, which has caused difficulties in interpretation and abusive practice by the Congress itself and by the President. This issue should have been overcome with appropriate regulation from Congress and a correct and precise exercise of its competences, in addition to firm case law from the courts, as the Supreme Court did in the celebrated case *San Luis Province (2002),* in which our highest court made a correct interpretation of the scope of the emergency and the use of decrees of necessity and urgency and of legislative delegation.

In terms of the principal idea of *modernizing and strengthening Congress*, we also see the decision of the convention as being correct through these main institutional changes:

(1) extension of the ordinary period of sessions;
(2) direct election of senators with a reduction of their mandate to six years and an increase of their powers in federal affairs;
(3) new procedure for sanctioning laws;
(4) the creation of new monitoring bodies, such as the General Auditing Office of the nation and the Ombudsman, with functional relations with Congress;
(5) the need for regulation by Congress of the decrees of necessity and urgency and of delegated legislation, through the action of the Permanent Bicameral Commission and control by the institutes of the legislative body;
(6) assigning of greater powers in the declaration of federal interventions;
(7) recognition of its competence to remove the chief of Ministerial Cabinet by vote of censure, and the need for this officer to appear monthly before each of the Houses to report; and
(8) recognition of its competence to grant constitutional status to human rights treaties.

These important reforms, to which I tried to add more powers to the Senate to grant agreements for the President's appointments, have not had the force that our political system requires, in accordance with republican principles. We are particularly concerned about the Congress's neglect to exercise its primary role in legislation and in monitoring.

The principal idea of *guaranteeing the independence of the judicial branch* was also, we believe, correctly implemented through these institutions:

(1) Council of the Magistracy,
(2) Magistrates Impeachment Jury, and
(3) Public Ministry.

These three institutions are operating, regardless of the problems seen particularly in the functioning of the Council of the Magistracy, from its excessive bureaucracy and conflicts of competence with the Supreme Court, and in addition to the recent change of its structure by Law 26.080 issued by Congress. We believe that this latest reform, which has given more weight to the government in the Council, has affected the aim of ensuring the independence of the judicial branch.

Regarding the *strengthening of federalism and municipal autonomy*, we strongly agree with the decisions of the constituent assembly of which we had the honour to be member.

We analyse this further in Part III of this monograph.[41]

---

41. For an extensive analysis, *see* Hernández (1997a).

The principle of municipal autonomy also has been established in its various institutional, political, administrative, economic and financial aspects as an obligation that the provinces must guarantee.

We believe that the most cursory comparison with other federations in the world shows us to have a quite appropriate design of federalism with significant devolution of power and recognition of local autonomy.

With regard to the *granting of a new status to the City of Buenos Aires*, we believe it was another of the great successes of the constituent assembly, asserting the decentralization of power and recognizing special autonomy for the city, that we devoted Buenos Aires to the status of city-state, such as Berlin, Bremen and Hamburg in German federalism.

Although the constitutional design was correct, in the regulation made by Congress based on Laws 24.588 and 24.620, the supreme rule of Article 129 was not respected and it is necessary to make the changes needed for its enforcement, which includes, among other issues, that the city should have its own judicial branch, in all jurisdictions, and its own Police and Fire Departments.[42]

On the *recognition of new rights and constitutional guarantees*, we believe that here too there is broad consensus on the constitutional design chosen by the Constitutional Convention. Here the aim was to deepen the humanist and personalist philosophy of the Constitution that makes human rights its most important object. And the reform has increased significantly the recognition of rights and guarantees, which now have their internal source and external source, that is, the internationalization of human rights.

Here too, the remarkable progress achieved in this matter can be seen in the light of comparative law, as well as the very serious difficulties for the effective observance of human rights in Argentina, as a result of the permanent violation of the law and unconstitutional use of the institutes of emergency.[43]

Finally, regarding the seventh principal idea, *strengthening the processes of both national and supranational integration*, we believe that the reform produced was also correct. The possibility was established not only to create Regions by the Provinces (section 124) but also to sign treaties of integration that would delegate powers and jurisdiction to supranational organizations by the Federal Government (Article 75, Clause 24). This was the appropriate way to advance integration in its various orders, as one of the routes on which there are least disagreements, to address the complex and varied situations presented by the competitive and interdependent world of today.

---

42. *See* Hernández (1997a).
43. *See* Part V, Ch. I of this work.

§6. Judicial Review of the Constitutional Reform: The *Fayt* and *Schiffrin* Cases

I. Unconstitutionality of a Constitutional Reform

33. We must ask ourselves whether there may be a reform of the Constitution that is unconstitutional.

We answer affirmatively, in light of the various discussions that have taken place in constitutional theory and in our own institutional history.

In constitutional theory, we should remember the debates between Carl Schmitt and Hans Kelsen in European law, between Marbury and Frierson in US law and between Linares Quintana and Cueto Rúa in Argentine law.[44]

Then, in our constitutional history, there is a remarkable degree of questioning of the constituent power as a result, in our view, of the lack of adequate political and legal culture, which prevented us during long historical periods from reaching the agreements required by the Constitution.

Indeed, the initial problem with the reform of 1860, made in violation of Article 30 of the text of 1853 prohibiting any reform in the space of ten years, marked the beginning of the debate on our constitutional status, which we feel was recently settled in the Constitutional Reform of 1994, after a protracted political and institutional path marked by deep disagreements.

Remember that we had to recur to the theses presented in the twentieth century by Sánchez Viamonte and Bidart Campos on the nature of the original constituent authority in 1860 in order to overcome the objection of the unconstitutionality of that reform. And after that, nearly all the subsequent reforms had the same fate, for example, those of 1949, 1957, 1972 and even that of 1994.[45]

Accordingly, we believe that the unconstitutionality of a constitutional reform can occur when the limits established for the exercise of derived constituent power are violated.

In relation to the control of constitutionality of a constitutional reform in our law, it is necessary to distinguish between the following: (1) those at provincial level and those at federal level and (2) the matters of procedure of the reform and the matters of substance.[46]

For us it is clear that in our system, as in the US system, that was our model in this matter: the control of constitutionality of federal constitutional reform should not be exercised by the established power because otherwise it would put the courts above the bodies that have been given that power on behalf of the sovereignty of the people in its highest expression. But this was not recognized by the Supreme Court in the *Fayt* case, which we discuss later.

---

44. *See* Ekmekdjian (1995:165); Linares Quintana (1953:143).
45. We refer to this in our speech in the Constituent Convention of 1994 on the legality and legitimacy of this reform. *See* Hernández: (1995a).
46. *See* Hernández (2001:41 and 2012a), in which we analyse the constitutional judicial review of constitutional reform in comparative law, starting with US law, which is similar to ours in this aspect. There we mention that, since the twentieth century, state reforms have been declared unconstitutional by the Supreme Court, which has never happened in relation to the reforms of the Federal Constitution.

However, as we held earlier, it is possible to review the constitutionality of constitutional reform of a Province or of the City of Buenos Aires because these are constituent powers of second degree or third degree, and so should be adapted to the bases established in that of first degree, the Supreme Federal Law.

34. With regard to judicial review of provincial constitutional reform, our highest Federal Court, the Supreme Court, is the most 'national' of the constituted authorities because it can review what is sanctioned in provincial constitutionalism, that of the Autonomous City of Buenos Aires and of the municipalities to ensure the supremacy of the Federal Constitution.

There are several cases here in which the Court has made a constitutional judicial review of various provincial constitutional reforms with the aim of verifying if they have invaded powers delegated to the Federal Government or violated rights guaranteed by the Constitution or to ensure the republican system established by the Supreme Law.[47]

II. *Fayt* Case and Its Constitutional Implications[48]

35. The 1994 reform incorporated in Article 99, Clause 4, paragraph 3 the following norm concerning the appointment of federal magistrates: 'Once they have attained the age of seventy five years, a new appointment, with the same consent, shall be necessary so that they may continue in office. Judges of that age or over shall be appointed for five years, and may be indefinitely reappointed by this same procedure.'

Likewise, the eleventh Temporary Provision declared:

> The expiration of the appointments and the limited duration foreseen in the present clause shall become effective five years after the modification, simultaneously with the law regulating the Council of the Magistracy and the Magistrates Impeachment Jury.

Article 110, in turn, coming from the original text, established that the judges conserve their positions as long as they are performing in good conduct as one of the guarantees of the independence of the judicial branch. And, as Gregorio Badeni has argued, an interpretation of this norm is required that is in harmony with this Article 99, Clause 4, paragraph 3.[49]

---

47. *See* the cases cited by Spota (2004).
48. This is the title of my book, before mentioned. *See* Hernández (2001 and 2012a).
49. 'Seeking to link the Articles 99 Clause 4 and 110 of the Constitution, we believe that the first regulates the procedure for appointing judges, setting a limit to their mandates at the age of 75, without prejudice to any new appointment. The second imposes the principle of unmovability during the period of that mandate.' Badeni (1998).

However, this rule was challenged in a judicial presentation made by a Minister of the Supreme Court itself, Dr Carlos Santiago Fayt, who finally obtained a favourable decision from his colleagues, originating one of the most important debates in Argentina on constitutional theory.[50]

We must emphasize that, in contrast to the attitude of this justice, another Minister of the Court, Dr Cesar Augusto Belluscio, resigned saying he was about to be 75 and also did not want to take advantage of the ruling that had been issued in the case of his colleague.[51]

This case takes its name from Court Justice Fayt, who raised an action for the declaration of unconstitutionality against these provisions, persuading the High Court to rule on the case on 19 August 2000, declaring: 'the nullity of the reform introduced by the 1994 reform convention in Article 99, Clause 4, paragraph 3, and in the 11th temporary provision, to Article 110 of the National Constitution'.[52]

The ruling, extremely important institutionally and unprecedented in the case law of the Court, considered actions by the derivative constituent power judicially reviewable and admitted the possibility of a declaration of nullity of the reformed constitution itself.[53]

A. *Foundations of the Court's Ruling*

36. Following is a synthesis of the foundations, in the order in which they were made in the respective considerations of the ruling.

In effect, the Court stated that it could exercise judicial control over the reform process of the Constitution[54] because the convention had exceeded its powers in that the issue was not enabled by the declaratory law, and it could not invoke its implicit powers.[55] It likewise declared that Congress had admitted in the pre-constituent law the possibility of the sanction of nullity[56] for cases such as this, in which the

50. *See* Hernández (2001:12–14 and 2012a), especially n. 2, where we list the authors who give opinions on the ruling in question. Dr Fayt himself also wrote a book (*see* Fayt, 2000:VII), aiming to provide, in his own words: 'the anatomy of the supporting arguments used by the parties in the action filed against the National State'.
51. *See Clarín newspaper*, Buenos Aires, 7 Jun. 2005.
52. *See* the ruling in *El Derecho*, 17 Sep. 1999. This was signed by the ministers, Drs Nazareno, Moliné O'Connor, Belluscio, Boggiano, López, Vázquez and Bossert, the latter two with their own vote and with partial dissidence, respectively.
53. Remember that the only case decided by the Court, in *Soria de Guerrero c. Bodegas y Viñedos Pulenta Hermanos S.A.*, 256:556, 1963, as a general rule had resolved not to review these situations, based on the non-justiciable political issues. *See* Bianchi (1999:2).
54. *See* Considerando 6 and Hernández (2001 and 2012a).
55. *See* Considerandos 7, 8 and 9 and *Ibid.*
56. *See* Considerando 10 and 15 and *Ibid.*

possibility of reviewing the immobility of the judges had not been included.[57] It also argued the irrationality of the reform made.[58]

B. Our Opinion Contrary to the Ruling

37. We consider this ruling of the Court unconstitutional and one of the most serious erroneous precedents of all the history of the case law of the Supreme Court.

We believe the ruling ignores the fundamental principles of constitutional theory on the constituent power, constitutional supremacy and constitutional judicial review.[59]

We agree with Konrad Hesse on the principle of 'functional correction', which indicates that the product of a Constituent Convention can be revised only by another Constituent Convention,[60] that is, by the same supreme hierarchy of popular sovereignty, and never by the established powers, since these are at a lower level, even though it is the judicial branch or even the highest Court of the country.

Violating this, as was done in the ruling, means disregarding the basic concept of popular sovereignty, the basis of the republican system and democratic legitimacy, represented in its highest expression by the Constitutional Convention.

We would also maintain that the law of Congress authorized the issue, and that it was a reasonable resolution of the convention to establish the new appointment after age 75 years, as is shown by comparative law.[61]

This case definitely signifies a 'breaking of the constitution', in Hesse's words, when he argues: 'wherever the interpreter imposes on the constitution he ceases interpreting it, to change it or break it'.[62]

The judges of the Court failed in their mission to be guardians of the Constitution, acting corporately, placing themselves above the constituent power and affecting the very essence of the democratic and republican principles that inform our rule of law.

This is why we need to assert the principles and limits of judicial review, to be able to correct such an erroneous precedent in the future.

Judges need to distinguish the broad possibilities of constitutional interpretation, without incurring deviations or abuses involving injury to the principle of constitutional supremacy or to the division of powers and the republican system.

The importance of judicial law and of case law cannot be ignored, that this cannot mean government by judges, since, together with Frankfurter, Corwin, Dworkin

---

57. *See* Considerando 11 and *Ibid.*
58. *See* Considerando 14 and *Ibid.*
59. *See* Hernández (2001 and 2012a).
60. *See* Hesse (1983:49). This position is also held by Linares Quintana (1953) and Vanossi (2000:127).
61. *See* Hernández (2001:80 and 2012a).
62. *See* Hesse (1983:52).

and Tribe,[63] we do not accept Hughes' idea that 'the Constitution is what the judges say it is'.[64]

C. *The* 'Schiffrin' *Case*

38. In the case 'Schiffrin, Leopoldo Héctor c. Poder Ejecutivo Nacional s./Accíon Meramente Declarativa', the Judge Leopoldo Hector Schiffrin challenged the reform of Article 99, Clause 4 of the National Constitution that imposes an age limit of 75 years for the exercise of the position. In the first instance, the nullity and inapplicability of the constitutional text was declared as held by the Supreme Court in the preceding '*Fayt*', Fallos: 322: 1616. The Federal Court of Appeals of La Plata confirmed this ruling. Against it, the National State filed an extraordinary appeal. The Supreme Court reversed the appealed sentence and rejected the claim in Judgment delivered on 28 March 2017.[65]

Then we refer to the majority opinion of the Supreme Court's Judgment, of great constitutional importance, which overruled the *Fayt* case, as we had been claiming it.

In relation to the limit of 75 years introduced by the reform, it is maintained that 'it does not affect the substance of the guarantee of immobility or, therefore, the architectural principle of judicial independence, since the immobility does not require a lifetime, but an institutional legal system that creates the necessary conditions for judges to perform well and legally, independently and without interference or pressure from external powers, in order to prevent the predominance of subordinate interests over the supreme interest of justice and the law'. [66]

On the same subject, the Supreme Court adds that '... it is an objective and impersonal limitation, which is clear from the purpose of the rule as well as the intention of the constituents'.[67]

---

63. *See* Tribe (1988:34–35), in which the author cites the contrary opinions to that of Charles Evans Hughes from the important jurists mentioned. We summarize their thoughts: Frankfurter (who was Chief Justice of the US Supreme Court) stated that 'the ultimate standard or criterion of constitutionality is the Constitution itself and not that of what we have said about it'; Corwin argued that this view 'supposes a kind of transubstantiation by which the court's opinion of the Constitution becomes the very body and blood of the Constitution'; Dworkin said that 'we cannot assume that the Constitution is always what Supreme Court says it is' because 'sometimes, even after a decision of the Supreme Court, one may still reasonably believe that the law is on one's side', and Tribe himself argues that 'the meaning of the Constitution is a matter of legitimate dispute and that the Court is not alone in the responsibility of giving meaning to that question. Rather, a variety of players must make their own constitutional judgments and have the power to develop interpretations of the Constitution which are not necessarily in agreement with that of the Supreme Court, such as the president, legislators, state courts and the general public'.
64. *See* Hernández (2001:86–90 and 2012a).
65. *See* CSJN, Fallos 340:257.
66. *See* Considerando 22, CSJN, Fallos 340:257.
67. *See* Considerando 23, *Ibid.*

In addition, the highest Tribunal said that this 'does not violate acquired rights', 'since no one has the right to maintain laws or regulations or their inalterability, and this doctrine is deepened when it comes to constitutional reform'.[68]

The Supreme Court expressed that the subject of the Constitutional Reform of Article 99, Clause 4 was qualified for its treatment in the Convention, by the Declaratory Law of the Need of the Reform No 24.309, that in its Article 3° included what refers to the updating of the attributions of the Congress and the National Executive Power. And for that reason the Court says that 'it is not possible to sustain with consistent foundations that the limits of the authorization conferred by the Congress of the Nation to the reforming Constitutional Power have been violated'.[69]

The Supreme Court states that: 'Although the regularity of the Constitutional Reform process is a judiciable issue, the standard of the broadest respect towards the activity of the Constitutional Convention that must be applied for its interpretation, and this has the support in a fact of singular importance: it is about the sovereign will of the people, expressed through an organ -the Reforming Convention- that has the highest degree of representativeness, since the citizens choose the conventional ones with full consciousness and knowledge that they will carry out immediately and concretely the mission of reforming the Fundamental Law.'[70]

And the Court adds respect to the function of the Judicial Power in charge of the control of the activity of the Constitutional Convention, with restrictive criterion, as it was done in the *Fayt* case, that 'it cannot be sustained in the principles of the division of powers on which the republican form of government is based, because it implies a high risk of interfering in the democratic process, altering the balance designed by the National Constitution so that, on the one hand, each one of the powers to remain within its sphere and, on the other hand, so that the constituted power does not leave without effect the sovereign will of the people expressed, through a Reforming Convention integrated by its elected representatives, in the Fundamental Law'.[71]

This criterion of maximum respect towards the constituent power is reaffirmed in this statement of the Supreme Court: 'The Judicial Power cannot analyze the convenience of the decisions of the constituents or ignore an essential budget of our democracy, according to which the National Constitution materializes a pact of national union among all citizens'.[72]

§7. The Principle of Constitutional Supremacy

39. The Constitution is the Supreme Law of a state, expressly ruling that all the norms of the system must be adapted to the fundamental norm, and it is necessary to safeguard this primacy.

68. *See* Considerando 25, *Ibid.*
69. *See* Considerando 20, *Ibid.*
70. *See* Considerando 10, *Ibid.*
71. *See* Considerando 11, *Ibid.*
72. *See* Considerando 12, *Ibid.*

The Argentine Constitution accepts this principle, setting a hierarchical order of its substance in Articles 31 and 75, Clause 22. Article 31 declares:

> This Constitution, the laws of the Nation enacted by Congress in pursuance thereof, and treaties with foreign powers, are the supreme law of the Nation; and the authorities of each province are bound thereby, notwithstanding any provision to the contrary included in the provincial laws or constitutions, except for the province of Buenos Aires, the treaties ratified after the Pact of November 11, 1859.

The 1994 reform of the Argentine Constitution in Article 75, Clause 22 expressly stated that international instruments take precedence over the laws. It also gave constitutional hierarchy to various international human rights instruments.

The Constitution also recognizes the processes of economic and commercial integration, regulating integration treaties in Article 75, Clause 24. According to this norm, these treaties may 'delegate powers and jurisdiction to supranational organizations under reciprocal and equal conditions, and which respect the democratic order and human rights'. And the same constitutional provision provides that in such cases 'the rules derived there from have a higher hierarchy than laws'. Thus, the existence of 'community rights' will also take priority over laws of internal rights.

Moreover, the National Constitution, the treaties and federal laws passed as a result of these prevail over provincial and municipal constitutions and laws.

Chapter 2. The Treaties

§1. Hierarchy of Treaties and Laws: Human Rights Treaties

40. As we have said, the 1994 reform of the Argentine Constitution in Article 75, Clause 22 expressly stated that international instruments take precedence over the laws. It also gave constitutional hierarchy to eleven international human rights instruments:

> The American Declaration of the Rights and Duties of Man; the Universal Declaration of Human Rights; the American Convention on Human Rights; the International Pact on Economic, Social and Cultural Rights; the International Pact on Civil and Political Rights and its empowering Protocol; the Convention on the Prevention and Punishment of Genocide; the International Convention on the Elimination of all Forms of Racial Discrimination; the Convention on the Elimination of all Forms of Discrimination against Woman; the Convention against Torture and other Cruel, Inhuman or Degrading Treatments or Punishments; and the Convention on the Rights of the Child … ..

These instruments, according to Article 75, Clause 22 of the National Constitution:'... in the full force of their provisions, have constitutional hierarchy, do not repeal any Article of the First Part of this Constitution and are to be understood as complementing the rights and guarantees recognized herein'.

Finally, it is included the possibility of granting the same precedence to other human rights treaties: 'In order to attain constitutional hierarchy, the other treaties and conventions on human rights shall require the vote of two-thirds of all the members of each House, after their approval by Congress.'

This is the situation of three Conventions with constitutional hierarchy: the Convention on Forced Disappearance of Persons, under Law 24.820 of 1997, the Convention on the Non-Applicability of Statutory Limitations to War Crimes and Crimes against Humanity under Law 25.778 of 2003 and the Convention on rights of persons with disabilities, under Law 26.378 of 2014.[73]

41. It should be noted that prior to 1994, the Argentine Supreme Court, in the case of *Ekmekdjian v. Sofovich,*[74] understood that the provisions of international treaties in force in domestic law were operative and have superiority over the laws.

This hierarchy is recognized for such documents, 'in the conditions in which they are in force'. Indeed, both the national doctrine[75] and the case law of Supreme

73. For Sagüès, the treaties mentioned in Art. 75, Clause 22 'are on the same plane as the constitution, even though strictly, from the formal point of view, they are not inserted within it' (Sagüès, 1997:1–222). Bidart Campos (2000c), in turn, has argued that these international instruments are part of the so-called bloc of constitutionality.
74. La Ley, t. 1992-C, 543 and ff.
75. *See* Ekmekdjian (1997).

Court, referring to the conditions of application of international treaties in Argentina, have indicated that they are the same as those that 'actually rule at the international level and particularly considering their effective enforcement by international courts competent to interpret and apply them. This is the basis [on which] ... case-law [of these international tribunals] should serve as a guide for interpreting the conventional precepts'.[76]

Thus, it is up to the Argentine courts 'to the extent of their jurisdiction, to implement international treaties to which the country is bound under the terms described above, since the contrary might imply the responsibility of the Nation towards the international community'.[77] In effect, the state would incur a violation of the treaty both when it applied an incompatible or contrary internal law, and when it omitted to apply it.[78]

42. It is worth remembering then which of these bodies are likely to issue pronouncements, observing as a 'guide' at the local level. Here we must look at the inter-American system and at that of the United Nations.

In the case of the American Convention on Human Rights (Pact of San José de Costa Rica), its currency includes that of its competent bodies:[79] the Inter-American Commission on Human Rights and the Inter-American Court of Human Rights (IACHR). Both bodies issue statements that affect national law and the respective authorities. A distinction must be made between the judgments, the advisory opinions and the provisional measures of the Court, which are obligatory, and the opinions of the Inter-American Commission, which, on the contrary, have given rise to a varying case law. In one case, the Argentine Supreme Court considered the opinions of the commission to be obligatory,[80] whereas in other cases, it varied.[81] Currently, it maintains the criterion of the obligatory nature of the decisions of the inter-American system.[82]

To sum up, 'when applying Argentine constitutional law, the local judge must know and put into effect also the Pact of San José de Costa Rica, and the interpretation given this by the Inter-American Court', in what is known as 'harmonizing interpretation'.[83] Thus, taking into account advisory opinion 13 of the Inter-American Court, 'not even a local constitutional interpretation may oppose the supranational case-law'.[84]

76. *See* C.S.J.N.: *Giroldi*, 7 Apr. 1995, L.L., t. 1995-D, 461 and 462, Considerando 11.
77. *Ibid.*, Considerando 12.
78. *See* Bidart Campos (2000b:418).
79. Article 33, American Convention.
80. *See* C.S.J.N.: *Bramajo*, 12 Sep. 1996, L.L., t. 1996-E, 408 and 409, Considerando 8.
81. When deciding in *Acosta* (1998) and fundamentally in *Felicetti* (2000).
82. In *Espósito Miguel*, of 12 Dec. 2004. *See La Ley, Suplemento de Jurisprudencia de Derecho Administrativo*, 19 Apr. 2005, 23–25.
83. *See* Sagués (1997:1–231).
84. Gordillo & Gordillo (1996:II:28).

§2. Treaties of Integration

43. Since the Constitutional Reform of 1994, Congress has the power, in Article 75, Clause 24, 'To approve treaties of integration which delegate powers and jurisdiction to supranational organizations under reciprocal and equal conditions, and which respect the democratic order and human rights.' We have noted previously that 'the rules derived therefrom have a higher hierarchy than laws'.

This constitutional norm distinguishes two types of treaties of integration, depending on whether they are signed only with Latin American states or with other nations. And according to that, the quorum for their approval varies. The Clause states:

> The approval of these treaties with Latin American States shall require the absolute majority of all the members of each House. In the case of treaties with other States, the National Congress, with the absolute majority of the members present of each House, shall declare the advisability of the approval of the treaty which shall only be approved with the vote of the absolute majority of all the members of each House, one hundred and twenty days after said declaration of advisability.

Finally, it declares that: 'The denouncement of the treaties referred to in this subsection shall require the prior approval of the absolute majority of all the members of each House.'

In 1991, Argentina signed with Brazil, Paraguay and Uruguay the Treaty of Asuncion, which established the 'Mercosur' (Southern Common Market). These states are full members. Venezuela joined in 2006, although its entry as a full member depends on the approval of the Congresses of the states' parties. Other Latin American states are associate members: Bolivia, Chile, Colombia, Ecuador and Peru. A process of integration is underway that has gone through various stages; its purpose is to promote the free exchange and movement of goods, persons and capital between the member countries and move forward to a greater cultural and political integration among its member countries and associates.

Chapter 3. Legislation

§1. Classification of Laws

44. Constitutional law also consists of norms not included in the formal text of the Constitution but that deal with constitutional topics.

Within a classification that is not exhaustive,[85] there are laws provided for in the text of the Constitution to complement it or regulate it, such as the Organic laws of political parties, in Article 38; of the General Auditing Office, Article 85; or of the Public Ministry, Article 120.

There are also special laws to govern in a single geographic area, such as the Federal Capital or the Autonomous City of Buenos Aires, Articles 3 and 129; or with respect to the creation of Provinces, Article 13; or for the purpose of recognizing constitutional status to human rights treaties, Article 75, Clause 22.

The base or framework laws[86] set the context in which certain policies have to be followed, which can be complemented with provincial norms, viz., on the subject of education, Article 75, Clause 19; on minimum budgets for protecting the environment, Article 41 and Article 42 on public services.

The law agreements should also be especially noted, such as on tax co-participation in Article 75, Clause 2,[87] where agreement is required of the Federal Government and of the Provinces.

Finally, we mention that Congress can enact National Codes on common legislation. Thus, Article 75, Clause 12 establishes as follows:

> To enact the Civil, Commercial, Criminal, Mining, Labor and Social Security Codes ... and particularly to enact general laws of naturalization and nationality for the whole nation ... as well as laws on bankruptcy, counterfeiting of currency and public documents of the State, and those laws that may be required to establish trial by jury.

45. According to the hierarchy of norms imposed by Article 31, decrees are also provided for in the Constitution as part of the powers of the Executive branch, always below the laws.

The Constitution authorizes four classes of decrees to be made:[88]

(1) reglementary, when Article 99, Clause 2 empowers the Executive to issue 'instructions and rules necessary for the enforcement of the laws of the nation, without altering their spirit with regulatory exceptions 'without altering their spirit with regulatory exceptions';
(2) autonomous, aimed at regulating the administration itself;
(3) delegated, as disposed by Article 76, by decisions of Congress;
(4) of necessity and urgency, following the provisions of Article 99, Clause 3.

85. *See* Sagüés (1997:I:114–118).
86. Incorporated in the reform of 1994.
87. *Ibid.*
88. *See* Sagüés (1997:I:489–497).

§2. DECREES OF NECESSITY AND URGENCY AND DELEGATED LEGISLATION

I. Decrees of Necessity and Urgency

46. The 1994 Constitutional Reform incorporated the following emergency institute into the Constitution in Article 99, Clause 3, paragraph 2:

> The Executive Power shall in no event issue provisions of legislative nature, in which case they shall be absolutely and irreparably null and void. Only when due to exceptional circumstances the ordinary procedures foreseen by this Constitution for the enactment of laws are impossible to be followed, and when rules are not referred to criminal issues, taxation, electoral matters, or the system of political parties, he shall issue decrees on grounds of necessity and urgency, which shall be decided by a general agreement of ministers who shall countersign them together with the Chief of the Ministerial Cabinet.
>
> Within the term of ten days, the Chief of the Ministerial Cabinet shall personally submit the decision to the consideration of the Joint Standing Committee of Congress, which shall be composed according to the proportion of the political representation of the parties in each House. Within the term of ten days, this committee shall submit its report to the plenary meeting of each House for its specific consideration and it shall be immediately discussed by both Houses. A special law enacted with the absolute majority of all the members of each House shall regulate the procedure and scope of Congress participation.

The Constituent Convention gave constitutional status, with severe limitations, as we shall see, to an institution that had long been exercised by the executive. In effect, the Presidents dictated decrees of necessity and urgency on some twenty notably exceptional occasions between 1853 and 1983.[89]

Subsequently, between the latter year and 1989, President Alfonsín issued about ten, particularly 1096/95 on the change of the currency from the Peso to the Austral, until the presidency of Menem, which was characterized by such an increase in their number that there was talk of 'government by decree'.[90]

89. Midón (2001:54–55) cites as examples those dictated by President Avellaneda when he ordered the temporary transfer of the Federal Government to the town of Belgrano because of the uprising of Tejedor in 1880 for institutional reasons and another declaring the state of siege for the same events.

90. *See* Delia Ferreira Rubio and Goretti Matteo (1994), who also noted that in the first four years of his first mandate, Menem dictated 308. Midón (2001:54) states that Menem used and abused the institution in such areas as taxation, wages, insurance, public debt, deregulation of transport, international trade, tax revenue sharing scheme, public services, state enterprises, retirement of personnel, transfer of real estate, industrial promotion and so on.

A significant sector of the publicist doctrine[91] supported the possibility of dictating these in the framework of the original Constitution of 1853 and 1860, whereas another sector to which we belong argued the contrary position.[92]

In terms of judicial case law, it should be noted that in the *Peralta* case, decided by the Supreme Court in December 1990, the use of these institutes of emergency was legitimated, regardless of the contrary doctrinal opinions that we share.[93]

It is thus understandable that the Constitutional Convention of Santa Fe and Paraná of 1994 regulates the institute, with text as noted previously of Article 99, Clause 3, a simple reading of which indicates that the aim was to limit these decrees as much as possible.

No other meaning can be read into the fact that:

(a) As a general rule, the executive cannot dictate in any case under pain of absolute and incurable nullity, issue provisions that are legislative in nature.
(b) Only when exceptional circumstances make it impossible to follow the ordinary processes for the sanctioning of laws can decrees be issued for reasons of necessity and urgency.
(c) But never in penal, tax or electoral matters or matters related to the regulation of political parties can decrees be issued for reasons of necessity and urgency.
(d) These decrees must be decided in a General Meeting of Ministers and signed by all the Ministers, as well as the Chief of the Cabinet and the President.
(e) A special procedure is required, subjecting the decree to the consideration of a permanent Bicameral Commission by the Chief of the Ministerial Cabinet, who must do so in person and within ten days of issuing it. In turn, the commission is obliged to present its decision to each of the Houses within ten days, to be dealt with expressly and immediately by the full House.
(f) Silence of the Congress is not admitted in the face of decrees of necessity and urgency because Article 82, also incorporated by the reform, established: 'The will of each House shall be expressly stated; the tacit or fictitious approval is excluded in all cases.'

Accordingly, the Constituent Convention established a criterion for the future that prevented the recognition of a decree by the inaction of Congress, as the precedent of the *Peralta* case had admitted.

91. *See* Midón (2001:55), n. 92.
92. *Ibid.*, n. 93. I expressed my opinion in my first bill as national deputy, presented on 19 Dec. 1991, which stated in its Art. 1: 'The decrees of necessity and urgency dictated by the Executive are absolutely and incurably null, whatever the circumstances on which they are based.' Art. 2 declared: 'The decrees of necessity and urgency dictated up to the entry into force of this Act may be ratified by law within sixty days after the entry into force of this Act.' In the Foundations, I explained: 'If the Congress does not defend absolutely firmly the faculties that are proper to it, in the face of the uncontainable advance of the Executive, the Republic will be in serious danger.' *See* Hernández (1995b).
93. *See* Midón (2001:54–57).

However, since agreements could not be reached in the Convention on the final aspects of congressional intervention, this had to be deferred to regulatory legislation, which was enacted Congress only in 2006, as Law 26.122.[94]

In institutional practice, no real change occurred because the executive continued dictating decrees of necessity and urgency in the presidencies of Menem as well as that of De la Rúa, Duhalde, Kirchner and Fernández de Kirchner, given the lack of reaction of Congress and the permissive attitude in the case law of the Supreme Court.

This issue of government by decree consolidated hyperpresidentialism and the lack of force of the Constitutional Reform of 1994.

II. Legislative Delegation

47. This institute was also incorporated into the text of the Constitution in the 1994 reform, in Article 76:

> The legislative powers shall not be delegated to the Executive Power save for issues concerning administration and public emergency, with a specified term for their exercise and according to the delegating conditions established by Congress. The expiration of the term foreseen in the previous paragraph shall not imply the revision of the legal relationships emerging from the rules issued as a result of the powers delegated by Congress.

The eighth Temporary Provision, also corresponding to this reform, declared: 'The pre-existing delegated legislation with no specified term for its application shall expire after this provision had been in force for five years, except for that legislation expressly ratified by the National Congress through a new law.'

Article 100, in turn, concerning the Chief of the Ministerial Cabinet, mentioning its functions, states in Clause 12: 'To countersign decrees about powers delegated by Congress, which shall be under the control of the Joint Standing Committee.'

Legislative delegation had already been admitted by the case law of the Supreme Court from the *Delfino* case of 1927 and was widely used throughout Argentina's institutional history.

Legislative delegation is the transfer of specific lawmaking competence by Congress to the executive in certain subjects and under specially set periods and conditions.

Regardless of the negative view of John Locke in these matters, European and North American comparative law, which would influence the Argentine system,

94. *See* all the process of incorporation of the institute of the constitution in Midón (2001:59–69); Ortiz Pellegrini-Aguirre (1995) and Pérez Hualde (1995). Law 26.122 has also been the object of fierce criticism, as it consolidates the permanency of the decrees when it requires their derogation by both Chambers of Congress.

steadily imposed this practice based on the assertion of the political leadership of the executive body over the legislature in contemporary politics.[95]

This advance of lawmaking powers of the executive branch was aggravated by the President in turn delegating powers to lower organisms, which ultimately resulted in the issuance of rules by the Federal Administration on Public Revenue, the Central Bank, the Customs and various ministries, and so on, further affecting the rule of law.

Moreover, the delegated legislation normally lacked any control by the delegating authority, that is, the National Congress.

Thus, we come to the Constitutional Reform of 1994, which incorporates the rules transcribed previously, with the aim of restricting and monitoring the exercise of this institute of emergency.

We agree with Badeni (2001:2) that the legislative delegation the constitution authorizes provides an exceptional and limited solution of restricted interpretation.

48. Nonetheless, the exercise of legislative faculties by the executive has continued, unconstitutionally.

Especially from the first presidency of Menem, a notable and uncontrollable advance of the executive over the Congress was seen through two institutes of emergency: the decrees of necessity and urgency and delegated legislation, and as we saw earlier, without adequate resistance or control by the legislature, in the first instance, or by the judiciary, which developed a generally vacillating and complacent case law.

So we come today to have more than 2,000 norms issued by executive bodies as delegated legislation during the emergencies of that decade, in addition to those issued after the enactment of Law 25.148 of 1999 and the latest arising from Laws 25.414 of 2001 and 25.561 of 2002.[96]

This staggering number of norms also indicates a deficient judicial culture and security, an apparent abandonment of its powers by Congress, which regularly sanctioned the respective delegating legislation.

In effect, the laws of emergency and of state reform (23.696, 23.697 and 23.982) sanctioned in the presidency of Menem starting in 1989 signified the beginning of delegated legislation, which was ratified by Law 25.148 of 1999, thus avoiding its revocation, as had been provided for, with the correct intention of ending these practices, in the eighth Temporary Provision of the reform of 1994.

To this was added the legislation delegating the laws of 2001 during the presidency of De la Rua (Law 25.414), which gave rise to severe criticism in the literature because of its size (50), and that of Zero Deficit (Law 25.453), and finally, in 2002, in the presidency of Duhalde (Law 25.561), which has produced the most

95. This, for a series of reasons that the distinguished Constitutional Law Professor of National University of Cordoba, César Enrique Romero (1963), explained long time ago.

96. Palacio de Caeiro (2001:3). The writer establishes 1,900 norms up to the sanction of Law 25.414, and so we increase to more than 2,000 those dictated to date, as those corresponding to Law 25.561 must be added to these.

serious, thorough and comprehensive legislative delegation possibly in our history, and has been described as unconstitutional by doctrinal views that we share.[97]

This law, in its Article 1, declares a public emergency and delegates powers in the following terms:

> To declare, in accordance with Article 76 of the Constitution, a public emergency in social, economic, administrative, financial and exchange rate matters, delegating to the National Executive the powers included under this Act until 10 December 2003, according to the foundations as specified below: 1) Proceed to the reordering of the financial system, banking and currency market. 2) Revive the economy and improve the level of employment and of income distribution with emphasis on a program for development of the regional economies. 3) Create conditions for sustainable economic growth, consistent with the restructuring of public debt. 4) Regulate the restructuring of obligations in process of execution affected by the new exchange rate regime established in art. 2.

The magnitude of the delegation made can be easily understood, going far beyond the provisions of Article 76 of the Constitution. Unfortunately, this law has been extended by Congress for sixteen years, until 2018.

97. *See* Hernández (2002:1:227–231); Pérez Hualde (2002a:17) and Padilla Miguel (2002:5).

Chapter 4. Constitutional Judicial Review: Case Law

§1. Origins in Argentina

49. The constitutional judicial review, as a manner of maintaining the supremacy of the Constitution, was born out of case law of the Supreme Court of the United States, and from there it was received by Argentine case law.[98]

Concerned about the rebellions occurring in the United States in the 1780s and 1790s, James Madison (US statesman, known as the father of the US Constitution) explained in *Federalist No. 10* that the new institutional order should be directed at preventing acts of factions and that factional behaviour represented trends proper to and inevitable in legislative assemblies. From this arose the institutional remedy to tackle this danger, through a judicial branch, with its function of constitutional judicial review of the laws.

Alexander Hamilton (US statesman), in turn, explained the judges' faculty of constitutional judicial review in *Federalist 78*:

> The interpretation of the laws is the proper and peculiar province of the courts. A constitution is, in fact, and must be regarded by the judges, as a fundamental law. It therefore belongs to them to ascertain its meaning, as well as the meaning of any particular act proceeding from the legislative body. If there should happen to be an irreconcilable variance between the two, that which has the superior obligation and validity ought, of course, to be preferred; or, in other words, the Constitution ought to be preferred to the statute, the intention of the people to the intention of their agents. Nor does this conclusion by any means suppose a superiority of the judicial to the legislative power. It only supposes that the power of the people is superior to both; and that where the will of the legislature, declared in its statutes, stands in opposition to that of the people, declared in the Constitution, the judges ought to be governed by the latter rather than the former. They ought to regulate their decisions by the fundamental laws, rather than by those which are not fundamental.

This excerpt provides clear justification for constitutional supremacy and of constitutional judicial review and also the justification of the principle of contra majority control of judges, who can review laws of the legislature, using the democratic argument of respect for the sovereign will of the people at its best, which is the Constitution itself.

Later, Chief Justice Marshall in the famous case of *Marbury v. Madison* in 1803 stated:

> It is a proposition too plain to be contested that the Constitution controls any legislative act repugnant to it, or that the Legislature may alter the Constitution by an ordinary act. Between these alternatives there is no middle ground. The Constitution is either a superior, paramount law, unchangeable by ordinary

98. *See* Hernández (2001 and 2012a), especially 39–75.

means, or it is on a level with ordinary legislative acts, and, like other acts, is alterable when the legislature shall please to alter it. If the former part of the alternative is true, then a legislative act contrary to the Constitution is not law; if the latter part is true, then written Constitutions are absurd attempts on the part of the people to limit a power in its own nature illimitable (see Gargarella, 1996:47).

These principles that arose in the United States (*see* Tribe, 1988) were and continue to be a foundation of the Argentine constitutional system (*see* Hernández, 2001 and 2012a). In this system, the Supreme Court has the final voice in matters of interpreting the Constitution. This criterion does not mean accepting the idea that the Constitution is what the judges say it is.[99]

Although in Argentina too the origin of this control was in case law, it is now based in section 43, as another of the great advances of the reform of 1994. The control is exercised by any organ of the judicial branch, whether federal or provincial, and so the system is called 'diffuse'.

For the control to proceed, there must, in principle, be a concrete 'case', initiated at the request of the interested party, although now ex parte is also admitted.[100] The effect of the declaration of unconstitutionality of the law or decree or act impugned covers the parts of the process, without affecting its validity. There is no erga omnes effect.

§2. Case Law Principles of Constitutional Judicial Review

50. Linares Quintana states regarding non-justiciable political questions (1998):

> Under the principle of separation of powers and according to the specific nature of the roles belonging to each of them, legislative, executive and judicial, under the constitution, the judicial branch has no competence to deal with *political questions*, the nature of which is foreign to the essence of the judicial function, and thus their elucidation is the exclusive attribution of the political powers: Legislative and Executive.[101]

Another essential rule for constitutional judicial review is that '*Public acts are presumed constitutional* insofar as, through a reasonable interpretation of the constitution, they can be harmonized with it.'[102]

Finally, regarding the principle on privative powers of the other Branches, it has been argued:

> When speaking of the *privative powers of the political authorities*, Legislative and Executive, one is not referring indistinctly to all those that have been

99. As we said in Ch. I of this First Part, commenting on the *Fayt* case.
100. As from the *Mill de Pereyra* case, according to the ruling of the Supreme Court of the Nation.
101. *See* Hernández (2001:59 and 2012a) and, in US law, Tribe (1988:107).
102. *See* Linares Quintana (1998:583) and Hernández (2001:69 and 2012a).

> assigned to them by the Constitution, but only to those specifically privative of them, that is, those powers that are proper, peculiar, unique and exclusive to them and that, therefore, by their nature are outside the control of the Judiciary ... [103]
>
> In the same way as in political questions, in the cases at hand, the political powers act with a wide functional margin, within their respective competencies set by the Constitution, and under their political responsibility ... Consequently, it is beyond the competence of the judicial branch to control the way in which the political powers exercise the powers given to them by the constitution privatively, and so if it had been empowered to do so, the principle of separation of powers would have ceased to exist, with the judiciary invading the orbit delimited for the action of the legislature and the Executive branch.[104]

In a similar line of thinking, our Supreme Court in the *Cullen c. Llerena* case in 1893 established that 'it is an elementary rule of our public law that each of the three powers that form the government of the Nation applies and interprets the constitution by itself, when exercising the powers that it confers on them respectively' (Ruling 53:431/434). Subsequently the Supreme Court would ratify this case law guidance in a long series of judgments.[105]

103. Linares Quintana 1998:719.
104. *Ibid.*
105. Hernández, 2001:73 and 2012a.

Part II. Form of Government

Chapter 1. General

§1. Representative, Republican and Presidentialist System

51. The National Constitution, sanctioned in 1853, established a representative, republican and Federal Government in section 1 and others, according to the pattern of the North American Constitution of 1787.

Regarding the representative system, the Constitution declared in section 22: 'The people neither deliberate nor govern except through their representatives and authorities established by this Constitution … .' However, we should point out that institutes of semidirect democracy such as the 'initiative' and 'popular consultation' were introduced in the Constitutional Reform of 1994 in sections 39 and 40.

The republican system and the separation of powers among the legislative, executive and judicial branches with checks and balances were established as well, with the aim of ensuring human rights and avoiding the concentration of power.

The President and Vice President of the republic were elected in an indirect way by Electoral College, with a six-year mandate and without immediate re-election, until the reform of 1994, which established a direct double-turn election, with a four-year mandate and the possibility of immediate re-election.

The legislative power is composed of two chambers: (1) deputies, representing the people and (2) Senate, representing the provinces and the Autonomous City of Buenos Aires.

The judicial power consists of the Supreme Court of Justice of the Nation and the other lower tribunals.

The system is presidential, based on the 1787 Philadelphia model but with some modifications that established a presidential system even stronger in its competences, under the influence of Alberdi (1852), following the precedent of the 1833 Chilean Constitution.[106]

106. The Argentine presidency had more powers than the US system in co-legislative matters and in the appointment of officials. When we speak of 'strong' presidentialism, we refer to the set of powers that the Constitution grants the president. In general, it can thus be argued that the presidency as an institution has been strongly based on the US model. But we can distinguish different gradations in Latin American constitutions, ranging from that considered strongest (specifically Chile) to those that have been attenuated by reducing powers, and especially by the incorporation of institutions typical of parliamentarism, such as Argentina, among many other cases noted by Valadés (2003 and 2007). There, the distinguished constitutionalist acutely reopens the debate started by political scientists such as Linz, Valenzuela, Sartori and Nohlen about presidentialism

52. Nevertheless, it is clear in our history, and especially now, that the executive power has always exceeded in the exercise of its attributions over the legislative, without adequate control from the judicial branch.

As we will see later, Argentine 'hyperpresidentialism' has affected the checks and balances and the federal system as well. Thus, a process of political, economic and social dependence of the provinces on the national sphere of government was consolidated. This situation was particularly stressed by the regular states of emergency we have had in our history.

§2. Political Parties and Participative Democracy

53. The Argentine Constitution, since its reform in 1994, recognizes political parties in section 38, regulating the core aspects of their organization and functioning.

Similarly, the Constitution also refers explicitly to the political parties in section 37, referring to positive actions for access to elected and party offices in function of gender; in section 54, establishing the system of electing national senators; in section 77, setting aggravated majorities for bills to amend the electoral system and that of political parties; in section 85, regulating the leadership of the General Auditing Office, which corresponds to the opposition political party with the largest number of lawmakers in Congress; and in Article 99, Clause 3, exempting from the decrees of necessity and urgency matters concerning elections and political parties.

Article 38 states:

> Political parties are basic institutions of the democratic system. This Constitution guarantees the free establishment and exercise of their activities, as well as their democratic organization and performance, representation of minority groups, competition for those standing as candidates for elective public positions, access to public information and communication of their ideas.

---

and parliamentarism in Latin America, tending towards the renewal of the former through the incorporation of institutions of the latter, in order to moderate the concentration of presidential power and rationalize its exercise.

The presidency can also be analysed in relation to the person occupying it, from the point of view of political reality. In relation to Mexico, we believe that the political 'weakness' of the presidents Fox and Calderon has been positive for the functioning of the republican system and the separation and balance of powers, because of the existing three-party system (PAN, PRD and PRI), which has strengthened Congress and increased the independence of the judiciary. For the same reason, I am opposed to the idea that presidents should also be head of their respective political parties.

Valadés (2007) classifies Latin American presidential systems into three types: traditional, transitional and democratic. And he characterizes them as follows: 'The traditional corresponds to the authoritarian exercise of power, highly concentrated in the person holding the title of president, with regard to which political and legal controls are not an effective guarantee for fundamental rights; the transitional corresponds to a stage of development where there are effective judicial controls, but where political controls have not reached full development; in the democratic, the political and legal controls are present.' The third type is found only in Chile, Uruguay and Costa Rica.

> The State contributes to the economic support of their activities and the training of their leaders. Political parties shall make public the source and destiny of their funds and assets.

Organic Law 23.298 establishes that only the political parties may run candidates for elective public office. This matter and party funding (Law 26.215) present problems on which debate is still open.[107]

54. The reform of 1994 signified a transition to participative democracy, in which there are other institutes of political and social expression. Among these, Article 42 of the Constitution mentions the rights of users and consumers, and declares: 'The authorities shall provide for ... the creation of consumer and user associations.' Also, in the same norm, it adds: 'Legislation shall establish efficient procedures for conflict prevention and settlement, as well as regulations for national public utilities. Such legislation shall take into account the necessary participation of consumer and user associations in the control entities.'

Similarly, Article 43 broadens recognition of non-governmental organizations and interest groups, enabling the collective injunction 'against any form of discrimination and about rights protecting the environment, competition, users and consumers, as well as about rights of general public interest', to 'the associations which foster such ends registered according to a law determining their requirements and forms of organization'.

§3. Institutions of Semidirect Democracy

55. The reform of 1994 also incorporated the institutes of semidirect democracy,[108] such as the popular initiative and popular consultation.

Article 39 of the Constitution gives citizens the right of initiative to submit bills in the House of Deputies, which, once the formalities required for its viability have been passed, must be specifically addressed by Congress within twelve months. The rule specifies that projects related to constitutional reform, international treaties, taxation, budget and criminal legislation shall not be the topic of popular initiatives.

This constitutional device should be consistent with other norms of the constitution, such as political rights (Article 37), the right to petition (Article 14) and the principles deriving from the sovereignty of the people (Article 33).

The law regulating the exercise of the popular initiative is Law 24.747, originating in a bill that was presented as a national deputy. The law states that, for it to proceed, among other requirements, the initiative must be signed by not less than 1.5% of voters gathered in at least six districts of the total of twenty-four.

---

107. *See* Hernández (2006b).
108. *See* Hernández (2003b:398–402 and 2006b:224–226).

56. The popular consultation is the faculty of the people to give their opinion by voting about proposals presented to them by legislative or executive bodies.[109] It is a mechanism through which, to some extent, the people participate directly in the preparation of acts of government, and it is characteristic of a model of participatory democracy.

In Argentina at the federal level, the first and only experience with this was in 1984, when the national executive consulted with the people on the negotiations with Chile on the Beagle Channel conflict.[110]

Article 40 enables the consultation in two forms: (1) binding or (2) nonbinding. The former must be convened by Congress at the initiative of the Chamber of Deputies; voting is obligatory, the law calling for it cannot be vetoed and the affirmative vote of the project by the people of the nation makes it law, with automatic enactment.

By contrast, the nonbinding referendum can be called by either the Congress or the executive branch, within their respective competences and in this case it expressly provides for non-compulsory voting. Law 25.432 of 2001 regulates the procedural aspects of this institute.

---

109. This term is frequently used to refer both to the popular consultation itself and to the referendum and the plebiscite. The first is not binding in its results, whereas the other two are binding. The referendum consists of consulting the electorate to express its opinion about a law; however, in our context, *plebiscite* has a different meaning more linked to political use, as has occurred in history with the cases of Napoleon, Juan Manuel de Rosas or Pinochet. *See* Hernández (2003b:398–402 and 2006b:224–226).

110. *See* Decree 2272, 25 Jul. 1984 (ADLA, XLIV-C, p. 2593).

Chapter 2. The Congress

§1. General Characteristics, Competences and Bicameral System

57. Argentina has a bicameral legislature called the Congress, comprising a Chamber of Deputies and a Senate. As the principal representative body, the Congress is responsible for expressing the will of the people and is the focal point for the democratic system.

The main functions of Congress include the enactment of all legislation in the following matters: (a) economic and financial issues, such as budget, taxes and so on; (b) the development of the nation; (c) substantive law, such as civil, penal, commercial and labour codes; (d) aboriginal people; (e) the organization of judicial power; (f) military powers; and (g) emergency powers.

In addition, the Argentine Congress may approve or reject treaties or order federal intervention in a province. It has extensive authority in relation to war and peace and must declare the need for constitutional reform.[111]

The Congress has implicit powers and the exercise of political control over the other two branches of government, including impeachment proceedings.

As in any presidential system, the Argentine Congress is elected independently of the executive branch, for fixed terms of four years in the case of deputies and six years in the case of Senators. As in other presidential systems also, however, a series of checks and balances affect the powers of Congress and the President. Thus, the President of Argentina attends the opening of sessions of Congress to report on the state of the nation; the President may extend the period of ordinary sessions and call for extraordinary sessions as well. The execution and promulgation of legislation necessarily lies with the President. The President also shares in the exercise of legislative power, in a number of familiar respects. In particular, bills passed by Congress must be approved by the President before they become law, and a presidential veto can be overridden only by a two-thirds majority of both Houses. More significantly, however, the President may, in 'exceptional cases', exercise legislative power by decree, albeit within both procedural and substantive limits now prescribed by section 99(3). And despite a general rule that legislative power shall not be delegated to the Executive, an exception is made in section 76 for 'administration and public emergency'.

58. In fact, although the importance of Congress and of the responsibility vested on it is undisputed, the centre of gravity of public power lies with the executive branch. The explanation lies in a range of interconnected factors: (a) interruptions in the constitutional order that have sometimes resulted in the closing down of Congress, as in the coups d'état of 1930, 1943, 1955, 1962, 1966 and 1976; (b) the leadership role that the executive branch typically assumes in emergencies and in the political process; and (c) the citizens' distrust of politicians produced the crisis of political representation that affects the prestige of Congress.

111. For a more detailed classification of the various roles of Congress, *see* Sabsay (2004:547–588).

Critically, however, they also include the succession of political, economic and social emergencies that have diminished the role of Congress, including constitutional procedures that have facilitated this process. Thus, under the two terms of President Menem, from 1989 to 1999, approximately 500 presidential decrees of necessity and urgency were made, related to emergencies and other special needs, intruding on the legislative sphere. And Congress itself has been all too ready to delegate its authority to the President, effectively waiving its responsibilities in the face of an executive prepared to rule by decree. Such an absence of a democratic and constitutional culture explains the failure of Argentina to maintain an effective and truly republican system, with appropriate respect for human rights.[112]

§2. The Chamber of Deputies of the Nation

I. Composition: Electoral System

59. The Chamber of Deputies is the House that is designed to represent the people of Argentina as a whole. According to Article 45, it is 'formed by representatives elected directly by the people'.[113]

Nevertheless, the federal system exerts a notable influence on the composition of the Chamber of Deputies, both legally and politically. Each of the provinces, and the City of Buenos Aires, constitutes a single electoral district, from which deputies are elected, using a system of proportional representation involving closed party lists. Deputies must have lived for at least two years in the province for which they are elected, and elections to fill a vacancy are called by the government of the province concerned. The number of deputies to which each district is entitled depends on the size of its population, subject to two qualifications: each province is entitled to a minimum of five deputies, according to Law 22.847, Article 3 of 1982, and reapportionment depends on the census, which is not required to be held regularly. In fact, there are 257 deputies based on the census of 1980, despite two more censuses in 1991 and 2001. As a result, the most populous provinces tend to be significantly underrepresented, detracting from the democratic character of the House. Even so, however, an alliance between deputies from the provinces of Buenos Aires (seventy members of the House), Cordoba (eighteen) and Santa Fe (nineteen) and the City of Buenos Aires (twenty-five) would deliver a majority capable of adopting or rejecting any legislation in the Lower House.

112. *See* Part V Ch. 2 of this book.
113. The officers subject to impeachment under Art. 53 are the President, Vice President, Chief of the Ministerial Cabinet, Ministers and Justices of the Supreme Court.

II. Requirements and Duration of Office

60. To be a deputy, it is necessary to have reached the age of 25, to have been four years a fully qualified citizen and to be a native of the province concerned or to have two years of immediate residence therein.[114]

Members of the Chambers of Deputies serve for a period of four years, with half the Chamber retiring every two years, and there is no limit to their right to seek re-election. In practice, however, there is a strong influence of the national political parties on the way in which candidates are chosen, facilitated by the closed list system.

Ironically, the political influence of provincial governments on the Chamber of Deputies undermines its capacity to defend either federal principles or provincial interests. Most political decisions are taken by the President, with the support of provincial governors, who depend economically on the Federal Government for fiscal co-participation. The Governors in turn can effectively decide on the list of candidates and control the voting behaviour of their members in the Congress. This abuse of presidential power, which has been termed 'hyperpresidentialism', has tended to subordinate both Congress and the provinces, weakening not only republicanism but also federalism itself.

III. Exclusive Competences

61. Like most such Houses, it has exclusive power to initiate bills imposing taxation.[115] In addition, bills for recruiting troops must be initiated in the Chamber of Deputies,[116] and impeachment proceedings also begin here.[117]

§3. The Senate

I. Composition, Electoral System, Requirements and Duration of Office

62. The Senate is designed as the federal chamber, representing the constituent units of the Argentine federation.

Most significantly, each Province and the City of Buenos Aires are equally represented in the Senate, regardless of population size, by three Senators, using the province as a single electorate.[118] The political party that secures the majority of votes takes two Senate seats in each province, and the party that secures the next highest vote takes the third.

To be elected senator, the following conditions are required: to have reached the age of 30, to have been six years a citizen of the nation, to have an annual income

114. Article 48.
115. Article 52.
116. *Ibid.*
117. Article 53.
118. Article 54.

of 2,000 'strong pesos' or similar revenues and to be a native of the corresponding province or with two years of immediate residence.[119]

Senators serve terms of six years and can be re-elected without limit. One-third of the Senate is re-elected every two years.[120]

The current composition of the Senate is the result of substantial changes made in 1994, before which each province was entitled only to two senators and senators were elected by the legislature of the province concerned. Since the Constitutional Reform of 1994, the election is direct and provincial citizens elect three senators. As in the United States, the election of senators was a competence of provincial legislatures and the change to a direct election meant more accordance with the principles of democracy and popular sovereignty.

Some Provincial Constitutions, including those of San Juan, Córdoba, La Rioja and Tierra del Fuego, still authorize provincial legislatures to instruct federal senators on matters related to their particular interests.[121]

II. Exclusive Competences

63. On the face of the Constitution, the Argentine Senate is a powerful Chamber. It must approve all legislation. It has functions of great institutional importance, including the trial of officials impeached by the Chamber of Deputies; the authorization of a declaration of a state of siege by the President; and consent to the appointment of a range of officials, including justices of the Supreme Court, ambassadors and higher officers of the armed forces.

In addition, since 1994, the Senate has the sole authority to initiate two forms of legislation with particular significance for the federal system: the fiscal co-participation agreements envisaged by Article 75(Clause 2) and laws providing for balanced development of the country, enacted pursuant to section 75(Clause 19).

64. In practice, however, the Senate is inhibited in the exercise of its authority by the same phenomenon of 'hyperpresidentialism' that affects the Chamber of Deputies. In consequence, it does not fulfil a federal role of the kind suggested for it by the Constitution, despite the changes to its composition introduced in 1994. Its failure to do so has been manifest in a range of contexts: federal intervention in provincial affairs or fiscal co-participation.

A notorious example is the handling of the critical question of fiscal co-participation, where private negotiations between the President and the governors have taken the place of public and transparent debate in the Senate, with wide participation involving elected representatives of the provinces, and this has long-term implications for the autonomy of the provinces as well as for the authority of the Senate. It is important to remember that since the Constitutional Reform of

119. *See* Art. 55.

120. *See* Art. 56.

121. Furthermore, the last two of these legislatures can request the Senate to remove senators who do not follow those instructions. Objections have been raised as to the constitutionality of these procedures because they could affect the authority and immunities of the legislative branch. No provincial legislature has attempted to use this competence.

1994, the Senate has the initiative on this matter and on the balanced development of the country, and we have had no legislation as yet. The Constitution stated in its sixth Temporary Disposition that the end of 1996 was the expiration term for the enactment of the new fiscal co-participation system.

III. President of the Senate: The Vice President of the Nation

65. The Vice President of the Nation is the President of the Senate. Each senator has one vote. The equality of votes is maintained by conferring the presidency of the Senate on the Vice President of Argentina, without a right to vote unless the votes of senators are tied.[122]

The Senate appoints a President pro tempore in the case of the absence of the Vice President, or when she/he holds the office of President of the Nation.[123]

§4. Provisions Applicable for Both Chambers

I. Impediments to Be Legislator

66. The Constitution establishes various kinds of impediments to the exercise of the position of legislator. On the one hand, it fixes disqualifications, that is, the inability to take a legislative position for lack of a requirement, for having a certain condition, for a crime or for unworthy conduct. Article 64 states in this regard: 'Each House shall be the judge of the elections, rights and qualifications of its members, as regards their validity.' Neither may the regular members of the clergy be members of Congress,[124] nor ministers of the executive branch, unless they previously resign their position.[125]

However, incompatibility between that of legislator and other activities is a legal impediment to exercising two or more functions at the same time: 'No member of Congress shall be appointed to any civil office or commission under the Executive Power, without the previous consent of the respective House, except for employments subject to promotions.'[126] And the Governors in representation of their own Provinces may not be members of Congress.[127]

122. Article 57.
123. Article 58.
124. Article 73.
125. Article 105.
126. Article 72.
127. Article 73.

II. Sessions: Quorum

67. Both Houses assemble, on their own account, every year in ordinary legislative session from 1 March until 30 November.[128] The quorum for each chamber to enter in session is the absolute majority of its members.[129]

The President of the Nation annually performs activities associated with the opening of the legislative session of Congress, with both Houses being assembled for this purpose, and reports on the state of the nation, on amendments promised by the Constitution, and on recommendations for consideration of measures she/he deems necessary and advisable.[130] Both Houses begin and conclude their legislative sessions simultaneously. Neither of them, while they sit, may adjourn its meetings for more than three days without the consent of the other.[131]

The President of the nation may extend the ordinary legislative session of Congress.[132] These 'prorogued' sessions may continue dealing with any bill that has been started in the same year.

The President of the Nation may also convoke an extraordinary legislative session, 'when some serious issue of order or progress so requires it'.[133] In this case, Congress can deal only with the matter for which the extraordinary session was called.

III. Parliamentary Immunities

68. Parliamentary immunities, also called 'privileges', may be collective or individual.

The collective immunities are privative competences of both chambers that each exercises separately.[134] It includes drawing up its own regulations and the exercise of disciplinary authority,[135] the acceptance of its members' resignations[136] and interpellation.

Another collective privilege is to be the judge of the elections, rights and qualifications of the legislators.[137]

69. Individual immunities are prerogatives enjoyed by legislators to ensure the free and independent exercise of the legislative function. For this reason, they neither violate the principle of equality nor are understood to be personal or corporative immunities.[138]

---

128. Article 63.
129. Article 64.
130. Article 99, Clause 8.
131. Article 65.
132. Articles 63 and 99, Clause 9.
133. *Ibid.*
134. *See* Sabsay (2004:558).
135. Article 66.
136. *Ibid.*
137. Article 64.
138. *See* Gelli (2001:446–448) and Sabsay (2004:560–561).

The Constitution expressly regulates immunities of opinion, arrest and process. The first means that 'No member of Congress may be accused, judicially examined, or disturbed for opinions expressed or speeches delivered by him while holding office as legislator.'[139]

Immunity from arrest means that 'No senator or deputy shall be arrested as from the day of his election until the expiration of his term, except when in fraganti surprised committing a crime deserving capital punishment or other infamous or serious punishment, in which case a summary report of the facts shall be submitted to the corresponding House.'[140]

Finally, by the so-called immunity of process, the 'stripping of immunity' may be performed, 'When a written complaint is filed before the ordinary courts against any senator or deputy.'[141] For this, 'once examined if there is enough evidence in a public trial, each House may, with the concurrence of two-thirds of the votes, suspend the accused party from his office and place him under the jurisdiction of the competent court to be judged'.[142]

As Gelli noted (2001:448), 'the scope, extent and limits of those powers derive directly from the provisions of those constitutional norms, so any law regulating them must pass a strict test of reasonableness'.[143]

IV. Interpellation and Reports

70. The Constitution declares that: 'Either House shall summon the Ministers of the Executive Power to receive such explanations or reports as it may deem necessary.'[144]

The chambers have the power to interpellate, that is, summon and interrogate ministers on matters of government. This is notwithstanding the fact, that, once the session of Congress is open, ministers must send 'a detailed report on the state of the Nation regarding the business of their respective departments'.[145]

However, different from the parliamentary system, the chambers do not have the power to remove ministers. But they can submit the Chief of the Ministerial Cabinet to a 'motion of censure' and if necessary remove him/her from the post.[146]

§5. Lawmaking Process

71. The will of Congress as a governing body is expressed in different ways, but mainly through the adoption of legislation, the procedure of which was the subject of several changes in the Constitutional Reform of 1994. It should be noted that the

139. Article 68.
140. Article 69.
141. Article 70.
142. *Ibid.*
143. In the year 2000 was enacted the Law 25.320 for the regulation of these institutes.
144. Article 71.
145. Article 104.
146. Article 101.

silence of Congress shows nothing because 'The will of each House shall be expressly stated; the tacit or fictitious approval is excluded in all cases.'[147]

The power to present bills for the Congress to deal with is broad. Article 77 establishes: 'Laws shall originate in either House of Congress, through bills introduced by their members or by the Executive Power, save for the exceptions established in this Constitution.'

Among these exceptions are those that are exclusive to each House, as we saw before, apart from the attribution of the executive to send draft ministries and budget legislation to Congress.[148]

Moreover, since the 1994 reform, citizens have the right of initiative to submit bills to the House of Deputies, which, after meeting some precautions, must explicitly deal with them within twelve months.[149]

Once the projects are presented, according to the rules of each chamber, they must be given 'parliamentary status', which means that the chamber accepted them and began their consideration to transform them or otherwise into law.

The chamber where the project entered becomes that 'of origin', and the other chamber becomes the 'reviewer', which is important at the time of adoption of the law if there are discrepancies between the two, according to Article 81.

The Constitution establishes that 'Bills modifying the electoral system and that of political parties shall be approved by the absolute majority of all the members of the Houses.'[150]

This issue is based on the great institutional importance of these matters, likewise excluded from the presidential faculty to dictate decrees of necessity and urgency,[151] so that the norms to be sanctioned on the subject achieve a high degree of consensus.[152]

72. The normal procedure for a bill is provided for in Article 78: 'When a bill is passed by the House in which it originated, it is sent to the other House for its debate. Once approved by both, it is sent to the Executive Power of the Nation for its examination; and if it is also approved, it shall become a law.'

According to the principle of checks and balances, proper to the republican system, the executive participates in the normal process of making and approving laws, promulgating them and having them published.[153] For this, the Constitution declares that 'Any bill not returned within ten working days is to be considered approved by the Executive Power.'[154] However, the Constitution limits this co-legislative faculty of the executive to this point because its own text states as a general rule that 'The Executive Power shall in no event issue provisions of legislative nature, in which case they shall be absolutely and irreparably null and void.'[155]

147. Article 82.
148. Article 100, Clause 6.
149. Article 39.
150. Article 77.
151. Article 99, Clause 3.
152. For an analysis of this issue, *see* Belisle (2008).
153. Article 99, Clause 3.
154. Article 80.
155. Article 99, Clause 3.

Moreover, the reform of 1994 introduced the possibility of chambers delegating to their committees the detailed treatment of a bill: 'After the general approval of a bill, each House is empowered to delegate to its committees the detailed approval of said bill with the absolute majority vote of its members.'[156] The composition, subject matter and working of the committees are governed by the regulations of each chamber.

73. It is possible that the opinion of each chamber may not coincide on a particular bill, and this issue is considered in Article 81 of the Constitution:

> If the bill were subject to additions and amendments by the revising House, the result of the voting shall be made known in order to state if such additions or amendments were made by the absolute majority or by two-thirds of the members present. With the absolute majority of its members present, the originating House shall approve the bill with the additions or amendments made or insist on the original text, unless the additions or amendments were made by the revising House with two-thirds of those members present. In such a case, the bill shall be sent to the Executive Power with the additions or amendments of the revising House, unless the originating House were to insist on the original text with the vote of two-thirds of the members present. The originating House shall not include new additions or amendments to those already made by the revising House.

In addition, the same section states that: 'No bill wholly rejected by either House shall be reintroduced in the legislative session of the same year. No House shall totally reject a bill originated in it and later added or amended by the revising House.'

74. We noted that the executive takes part in the process and has ten days to express its will. At this point, it may happen that, not sharing the opinion of the parliament, the executive vetoes the bill sanctioned totally or partially.

So, 'If a bill is totally or partially rejected by the Executive Power, it shall return with the objections to the originating House; the latter shall reconsider it and if it is confirmed by a majority of two-thirds of the votes, it shall be sent again to the revising House. If both Houses approve it by such majority, the bill becomes a law and is sent to the Executive Power for promulgation,' but 'If the Houses differ as to the objections, the bill cannot be reintroduced in the legislative session of that year.'[157]

There may also be a partial veto, with certain precautions: 'When a bill is partially rejected, the remaining part shall not be approved. However, non-vetoed parts may only be promulgated if they have normative autonomy and if their partial approval does not alter the spirit or the unity of the bill approved by Congress. In this case, the procedure foreseen for decrees of necessity and urgency shall be applicable.'[158]

156. Article 79.
157. Article 83.
158. Article 80.

§6. CONTROL ORGANS

I. General Auditing Office of the Nation

75. The legislative power is exclusively empowered to exercise the external control of the national civil service regarding its condition and its economic, financial and operative aspects.

The review and opinion of the legislative power about the performance and the general situation of the national civil service are based on the reports of the General Auditing Office of the Nation, an advisory body of Congress with functional autonomy. The chairperson of this office is appointed on the recommendation of the opposition party with the largest number of members in the Congress, according to Article 85 of the National Constitution.

It is responsible for the control of the legal aspects, management and auditing of all the activities of the centralized and decentralized civil service, as well as of other powers granted by law. It takes part in the approval or rejection of the revenue and investment accounts of public funds.

II. Ombudsman

76. Another control organ created in the 1994 reform is the national Ombudsman. The mission of the ombudsman is the defence and protection of human rights and other rights, guarantees and interests sheltered under the Constitution and the laws, in the face of deeds, acts or omissions of the administration, as well as the control of public administrative functions. It is an independent authority created within the sphere of the National Congress. It operates with full autonomy and without receiving instructions from any other authority.[159]

The Ombudsman has the capacity to be a party in a lawsuit and may file injunctions in cases of collective or diffuse rights.[160]

The Ombudsman is appointed and removed by Congress with the vote of two-thirds of the members present from each House, has the immunities and privileges of legislators, holds office for the term of five years and may only be reappointed on one occasion.

159. Article 86.
160. Articles 86 and 43.

Chapter 3. The Executive[161]

§1. Composition, Electoral System, Requirements and Duration of Office

77. The Executive power of Argentina is vested in a citizen with the title of 'President of the Argentine Nation.'[162] For this reason, most of the doctrine considers the executive branch a unipersonal organ. But, in the case of illness, absence, death, resignation or removal of the President from office, the executive power is devolved upon the Vice President of the Nation.[163]

Both the President and the Vice President are directly elected, by double ballot, using the entire country as a single electorate. The President and the Vice President are elected for a fixed four-year term but may only be re-elected once for a consecutive term.

Prior to the constitutional changes of 1994, the President of Argentina was elected indirectly, through an Electoral College. As in the case of the Senators, the National Constitutional Convention changed the system in accordance with the principles of democracy and popular sovereignty. However, some scholars take the view that the new arrangements have a detrimental effect, diminishing the influence that the smaller provinces were able to exert through the Electoral College, and thus increasing the potential for presidential elections to be decided by only four or five large provinces. Others, including myself, believe that the current system should be maintained on the basis that it is far more democratic than the previous one and that to the extent that there is a problem the solution lies in changing the high levels of population concentration in the country by strong policies.

Article 89 set the requirements to be elected President or Vice President of the Nation: 'it is necessary to have been born in the Argentine territory or to be the son of a native-born citizen if born in a foreign country and to have the other qualifications to be elected Senator'.

§2. Competences

78. The powers of the President, according to the present Constitution, are regulated in Articles 99 and can be classified according to Sabsay (2004b:618) as: co-legislative (Clauses 3, 8 and 9), regulatory (Clauses 2 and 3), appointment and dismissal of officials (Clauses 4, 7 and 19), pensions (Clause 6), financial powers (Clause 10), military powers (Clauses 12–15), representation before the international community (Clause 11) and emergency powers (Clauses 5, 16 and 20).

The Constitution gives co-legislative-type powers to the executive; it can introduce bills, in addition to promulgating and publishing those sanctioned by Congress (Article 99, Clause 3). It also has the faculty to veto laws (Article 83).

161. *See* Antonio María Hernández, Ch. XVII 'El Poder Ejecutivo', in 'Derecho Constitucional', Director Antonio María Hernández, La Ley, Buenos Aires, 2012, Tomo II, p. 129 and ff.
162. Article 87.
163. *Ibid.*

In addition, the President must perform annually the opening of the ordinary sessions of Congress, give an account of the state of the nation (Article 99, Clause 8) and may extend the ordinary sessions and summon extraordinary sessions (Article 99, Clause 9).

The President has regulatory powers to execute the laws (Article 99, Clause 2) and exceptionally may issue decrees of necessity and urgency, 'when due to exceptional circumstances the ordinary procedures foreseen by this Constitution for the enactment of laws are impossible to be followed, and when rules are not referred to criminal issues, taxation, electoral matters, or the system of political parties' (Article 99, Clause 3).

In addition, the Congress may delegate to legislative faculties in certain matters of administration or of public emergency, for a set period and according to the conditions Congress may establish (Article 76).

The President appoints the public officers. It is necessary the agreement of the Senate for the cases indicated, according to Article 99 (Clauses 4, 7 and 19).

§3. Vacancy

79. The cases of temporary absence and vacancy in the post, occurring before assuming office or during the exercise of the mandate, have been considered in various ways. Some alternatives are set in the Constitution.[164] Others are governed by laws.[165]

Among the possible situations, death, destitution, resignation, absence, suspension or other impediment are mentioned. If the absence is from any of the first three cases relating to permanent impediments, the functions of the office pass to the Vice President, who exercises them during the remainder of the constitutional period. In cases of absence, suspension or other temporary impediment, however, the Vice President assumes the presidential functions until the cause ceases to exist.

Another possibility is the simultaneous separation or impediment of both President and Vice President. In this case, the office is exercised by the provisional President,[166] until Congress, meeting in legislative assembly, appoints the official[167] who will take charge of the executive.

§4. Chief of the Ministerial Cabinet

I. General Characteristics: Competences

80. The position of Chief of the Ministerial Cabinet was incorporated by the Constitutional Reform of 1994. The President appoints the Chief of the Ministerial Cabinet.

164. Article 88.
165. Law 20.972 and its amendment by Law 25.716 (2003).
166. Article 58.
167. According to the law, this must be a Senator, National Deputy or Provincial Governor.

The functions of the office, as described in Article 100 of the Constitution, are as follows: general administration of the country (Clause 1); appointment of administrative employees, except those that are the responsibility of the President (Clause 3); preparation of cabinet meetings; submission of certain categories of bills to Congress; and collection of taxes and implementation of the budget (Clause 7).

The Chief of the Cabinet has special responsibilities in relation to emergency decrees. She/he must countersign them, together with other ministers and personally submit such decrees to the Joint Standing Committee of Congress within ten days of their promulgation (Clauses 12 and 13).

Other functions are described in Articles 100 of the National Constitution: to issue regulations or acts (Clause 2); to exercise the functions delegated by the President (Clause 4); to coordinate, prepare and convene meetings of cabinet ministers, presiding in case of absence (Clause 5); and to send to Congress the bills of Ministries and of the national budget (Clause 6).

She/he also has similar responsibilities to the Ministers in terms of the department but, unlike them, is politically responsible to the Congress (Article 100).

II. Presence in the Chambers

81. Unlike ministers, the Chief of the Cabinet is politically answerable to Congress, attending sessions once a month, and alternating between Houses in order to inform the Congress about progress that the government is making.

The chief can be censured by Congress and may be removed from office by a majority vote of members of each House. In these respects, the position seems to be similar to that of Prime Minister in a parliamentary system. The similarity is superficial, however.

In reality, the position of Chief of Cabinet is that of a coordinating minister in an essentially presidential system, which has been designed to impose some greater structure on the power of the President and not to change the nature of the system. Its incorporation in the 1994 reform aimed to attenuate our presidentialism and not to change the system towards one that is semi-presidentialist or parliamentary.

The Chief of Cabinet answers to the President, who makes the initial appointment and may terminate it as well. Similar arrangements, with similar objectives, have been put in place in other presidential systems in Latin America.[168]

Despite the original intentions, more than ten years after the introduction of the position of Chief of Cabinet, it seems that it has had no significant effect in diminishing the strong form of presidentialism in Argentina.[169]

---

168. *See* Valadés (2003 and 2007), who analyses the cases of Peru (which was the first to introduce this type of institutions), Argentina, Bolivia, Colombia, Uruguay, Costa Rica, Ecuador, Guatemala, El Salvador, Honduras, Nicaragua, Panama, Paraguay and Venezuela, in Latin America, which have renewed presidentialism in their constitutional reforms, within forty-eight cases observed in comparative constitutional law, which helps him to give a basis to his naming it 'parliamentarized presidentialism'. He also argues that a presidentialization of parliamentary systems can be seen.
169. Chiefs of Cabinet have been politicians of the same party as the President and their importance was relative. In fact, this function is similar to a Minister of Coordination of a presidential system, rather than a Chief of Cabinet of a parliamentary system.

§5. The Ministers

82. The President appoints the Ministers. They countersign and thus give legal effect to the actions of the President[170] and take responsibility for administration of government departments.

Ministers are not members of Congress, although they may attend meetings, may be summoned by either House, must submit reports to Congress annually and are individually liable for their own decisions and collectively liable for joint ones.[171]

§6. Hyperpresidentialism

83. We need to explain the term *hyperpresidentialism*, both in Argentina and in other countries of the region.

For us, this phenomenon is characterized by the concentration of power in the President, beyond the remit established by the Constitution, to the detriment of the separation and balance of powers and the principles of constitutional democracy. Nino (1992a) studied this serious institutional pathology that causes immeasurable negative effects for the political and legal system and for an open society, presenting the following three sections from an interdisciplinary point of view:[172] (a) 'Current organization of power in Argentina',[173] with emphasis on constitutional law, which analysed the hyperpresidentialism in context, with the hypertrophied presidency, the weakening of Congress, the system of political parties and the electoral system, the process of submission of the administration of justice, the relative decline of federalism and of corporative bodies; (b) 'Evaluation of Argentine hyperpresidentialism from the standpoint of democratic legitimacy',[174] with emphasis on philosophy, which discussed issues such as the dispersal of sovereignty, deficient processing of consensus, the issues of imperfect mediation and political apathy and the impoverishment of public debate; and (c) 'Evaluation of Argentine hyperpresidentialism from the viewpoint of its stability and efficacy',[175] with emphasis on political science, discussing stability in relation to the personalization of power, the rigidity of the system and escape valves, blockages between the powers of the state and the dynamics of confrontation and the difficulty to form coalitions and then the effectiveness of hyperpresidentialism.

Referring to the hypertrophied presidency, according to the original constitutional text of 1853, that is, prior to the reform of 1994, he argued:

170. In this matter, the National Constitution was influenced by French legislation.
171. The number of ministers depends on the respective law and each presidency generally changes it. The will of the President establishes whether there is a Cabinet meeting. During the Néstor Kirchner Presidency there were not cabinet meetings. It was another example of our hyperpresidentialism.
172. *See* Nino (1992a), especially Ch. III, 'Organización del Poder'.
173. *Ibid.*, 497–569.
174. *Ibid.*, 569–617.
175. *Ibid.*, 617–653.

> This cursory review of the powers that the Presidents steadily acquired by a broad interpretation of constitutional provisions, by the surrender of the other branches of government, or by a straightforward exercise of political muscle, shows that, from the policy point of view, the Argentine president is, as Alberdi predicted, a true king, although unlike what he meant, his kingly powers have not prevented the instability of governments and abuse of power against the rights of citizens. It also confirms, with the distortion of the spirit and often of the texts of the constitution, in the granting and assumption of extraordinary powers by the President, the tendency to legal anomia that has been a constant in our political and institutional practice, even in periods de jure. (Nino, 1992a:529)

In his acute vision of hyperpresidentialism, Nino also pointed out the problems of corporatism, which he considered very important for understanding Latin American politics because of its association with the political regimes, such as bureaucratic authoritarianism, and with ideologies, such as populism. And he believed that 'the corporatization of the Argentine State has been obvious', noting the actions of the armed forces to take power as well as that of the Catholic Church and unions; and the economic system for the granting of privileges, monopolies and subsidies to certain groups of state contractors (Nino, 1992a:562–566). That is why he considered our democracy 'corporatist' and far from the correct model, which he defended, of 'deliberative' democracy (Nino, 1992a:605).

We think that his concepts are still valid today, and in particular we note that the problem of corporate hyperpresidentialism remains the most serious of our constitutional system, because after the 1994 reform, which incorporated institutions to mitigate it, the violation of the letter and spirit of the constitution is more clearly seen.[176]

Nowadays it is possible to observe a *political change after the 2015 Presidential election* because President Mauricio Macri has no majority in both Chambers of Deputies and Senate.

Under our point of view, this election results meant a great possibility for the democratic future of the country, so we encourage deepening the dialogue, to find the solutions of the structural problems suffered by Argentina.

We have reiterated in such a sense that the real change means in the first place a closer link between politics and ethics, to move away from the unfortunate phenomena of structural corruption, enhanced by impunity, which has characterized our low institutional quality.[177]

In relation to Latin America, it is true that the de facto governments contributed to the consolidation of hyperpresidentialism. But this pathological deformation of the institutions can also be seen in governments elected by the people. This is what

176. Particularly in the Presidencies of Menem, Kirchner and Fernández de Kirchner. Some scholars wrote on the establishment of a hegemonic presidency. *See* Botana (2007) and Bianchi (2007).

177. See Antonio María Hernández, 'Fortalezas y debilidades constitucionales. Una lectura crítica en el Bicentenario', Abeledo Perrot, Buenos Aires, 2012, where I analyse the matters of corruption, impunity and violence. We agree in addition, with Guillermo O Donnell and Carlos Nino reflections on the delegative and corporative characteristics of our democracy, that urge modify.

has been happening in Argentina for some time according the analysis as we have done. And this is what is seen in other countries of Latin America, such as Venezuela, Ecuador, Bolivia and Colombia.[178]

It is essential for us to affirm the trend towards attenuated, rational and controlled presidentialisms, which is seen in the constitutional reforms occurring in Latin America, and also the need to consolidate the good functioning of republican systems, with separation and balance of powers, to achieve open and democratic societies with an increase in constitutional culture and legality.

178. We also include Mexico in this list during the government of the PRI as a hegemonic party until the late twentieth century, but not now, because the existing three-party system has meant a significant institutional and democratic step forward for the country, especially in strengthening the Congress.

Chapter 4. The Judiciary

§1. The Federal Judicial Power

I. Organization and Competences

84. In the Argentine federation, there is both a Federal Judiciary and a judiciary for each Province and the Autonomous City of Buenos Aires.[179] The judicial branch of the nation is made up of the Supreme Court of Justice of the Nation and the other lower courts, as provided by the Constitution in Article 108.

The last federal Constitutional Reform of 1994 incorporated new institutions: the Council of the Magistracy, the Magistrates' Impeachment Jury and the Public Ministry, in Articles 114, 115 and 120.

'Federal' justice is limited, of exception and exclusive, with its competence established in Articles 116 and 117 of the National Constitution and in the respective regulatory statutes.

The first norm declares:

> It corresponds to the Supreme Court and to the lower courts of the Nation to know and decide in all the cases related to points governed by the Constitution and by the laws of the Nation, with the reservation made in Article 75 Clause 12; and by treaties with foreign nations; all cases concerning ambassadors, public ministers and foreign consuls; cases related to Admiralty and maritime jurisdiction; matters in which the Nation shall be a party; actions arising between two or more provinces; between one province and the inhabitants of another; between the inhabitants of different provinces; and between one province or the inhabitants thereof against a foreign State or citizen.

Article 117, in turn, establishes the original and exclusive competence of the National Supreme Court of Justice, restricted only to cases concerning Ambassadors, Ministers and foreign Consuls and those in which a Province is a party.

85. It also includes matters arising under the Constitution and under national laws except, importantly, the codes enacted pursuant to Article 75, Clause 12, in relation to which jurisdiction is apportioned between federal and provincial courts depending on their 'respective jurisdictions for persons or things'.

Then, in virtue of this norm of the Constitution, 'provincial' justice intervenes in cases of 'ordinary' law, to apply the underlying codes (civil, commercial, penal, labour, mining, etc.), which, in our constitutional order, are sanctioned by the National Congress, in contrast to the US precedent, where it corresponds to the States. One of the main competences of the Provinces is to sanction the respective procedural codes.

The highest Court of the Nation also has competence through appeal – ordinary and extraordinary – to ensure the constitutional supremacy embedded in Article 31

---

179. *See* Art. 5, requiring each province to enact its own constitution 'ensuring the administration of justice', and Art. 129 related to the Autonomous City of Buenos Aires.

of the National Constitution, and in consequence, can review all the acts or norms that fail to recognize it, whether from federal, provincial or municipal authorities, executive as well as legislative or judicial.

There is a possibility of the existence of different interpretations of the jurisdictions and to prevent it, there are some solutions, such as the following: (a) an authoritative interpretation of the Supreme Court of Justice in federal cases by extraordinary appeal, (b) plenary meetings of Courts of Appeals or (c) the National Penal Cassation Court. However, in some cases, there is a tendency to forum shop.

Both federal and provincial courts interpret and apply the National Constitution to cases otherwise falling within respective jurisdictions, but the final interpreter is the Supreme Court.

86. The federal jurisdiction is exercised by federal courts below the Supreme Court of Justice.[180]

There are federal judges of first instance and courts of appeal all over the country. The Congress is empowered to enact the legislative provisions devoted to federal justice administration.

87. The National Supreme Court of Justice is the head of the federal judicial branch and the final and irrevocable interpreter of the National Constitution.

Nonetheless, Argentina is subject to the judicial system of the Inter-American Commission and Court of Human Rights, as the American Convention on Human Rights (Pact of San José de Costa Rica) has constitutional standing in Argentina, according to Article 75, Clause 22 in its current conditions.

Thus, in virtue of Article 64.2 of this international instrument, the Inter-American Court, in exercise of its consultative competence, when requested by a Member State of the Organization of American States (OAS), can issue opinions about the compatibility between any of its domestic laws – for example, a Provincial Constitution – and the interpretation of this Pact or other Treaties concerning

180. The federal judicial branch has 890 magistrates and prosecutors in all areas, whereas there are approximately 4,500 in the Judicial branches of the Provinces and of the Autonomous City of Buenos Aires, but these figures do not sufficiently show the exceptional character of federal justice because magistrates and prosecutors are included there who should have been transferred to the judicial branch of the Autonomous City of Buenos Aires. This transfer, from the former national justice of the Federal Capital (in civil, commercial, labour and penal matters) to the justice of the Autonomous City of Buenos Aires, provided for in Art. 129 of the National Constitution, has not yet taken place. The Federal Government is thus still responsible for more than 500 magistrates corresponding to the latter jurisdiction. When Law 24.588 (the so-called Law of Guarantees of Federal Government while the City of Buenos Aires continues to be the Capital, which we consider unconstitutional as violating the previously mentioned Art. 129) is modified, then the number of truly ‘federal’ magistrates and prosecutors will be significantly diminished, with more than 500 of these being transferred to the common or ordinary justice, under the judicial branches of the twenty-three provinces and the Autonomous City of Buenos Aires. The federal judicial branch at present has 274 appellate judges and 354 examining magistrates of the Autonomous City of Buenos Aires, including the ‘federal’ magistrates and those who were previously called ‘national’ magistrates in civil, commercial, penal and labour matters. In the interior of the country, however, the federal judicial branch has 172 federal appellate judges and ninety-three examining magistrates. *See* Antonio María Hernández, ‘La Ciudad Autónoma de Buenos Aires y el fortalecimiento del federalismo argentino’, Jusbaires, Buenos Aires, 2017, and Hernández (1997a).

the protection of human rights. It can likewise dictate judgments obliging resolutions dictated by the Member States to be modified.

88. The main function of the courts is to exercise judicial review, the exclusive competence of the judicial branch.

Judges must apply, in the first place, the Constitution. They can declare the unconstitutionality of any rule or act of the legislative or executive branch.

Not only the Supreme Court of Justice or the higher courts of the provinces exercise control over constitutionality but also all the federal or provincial judges, since our system is diffuse, as in the US case.[181] It derives from this that the most important function that the judges have is that of executing this control, which presents different characteristics in the federal and provincial orders.

In the control of federal constitutionality, the judgment declaring unconstitutionality is limited to the concrete case because the norm continues in force. The usual procedural route is indirect or incidental, although since 1985, the Supreme Court declared that there are also direct actions of unconstitutionality such as the injunction (amparo), habeas corpus, habeas data and the declarative action of certainty of Article 322 of the Code of Civil and Commercial Procedures of the Nation.

In relation to active legitimation, after the Constitutional Reform of 1994, the Ombudsman and the associations depending on these purposes have been added to the current owner with a right or legitimate interest, in defence of collective or diffuse interests, as determined in Article 43 of the National Constitution.

II. Federal Judicial Review

89. The Supreme Court of Justice, as the highest court of the Argentine federation and the final and irrevocable interpreter of the National Constitution, is able to perform constitutional judicial review even over the laws or acts of the provincial or municipal organizations. And the most commonly used means for doing this is the extraordinary federal review, which carries competence through this Court's extraordinary appeal.

The review proceeds in the cases regulated by Article 14 of Law 48 through its three Clauses:

> 1) when the case raises the issue of the validity of a treaty, a law of Congress or of an authority exercised in the name of the Nation and the judgment has been against its validity; 2) when the validity of a provincial law, decree or authority has been questioned as being opposed to the national Constitution, to treaties or laws of Congress, and the judgment has been in favor of the validity of the provincial law or authority; 3) when the understanding of any clause of the Constitution, or of a treaty, law of Congress or a commission exercised in the name of a national authority has been questioned and the judgment is against the validity of the title, right, privilege or exemption based on said clause and is subject of the dispute.

181. *See* Bianchi (2002).

This means that for the appeal to proceed there must be an 'issue' or 'federal case' and that these can be divided into 'simple' or 'complex', depending on whether it is a case of pure and simple interpretation of the Constitution or a treaty or of a federal law or of a conflict between norms of whatever kind with the Constitution. Complex federal issues have, in turn, been classified into 'direct' or 'indirect', depending on whether the conflict directly arises between an infra-constitutional standard or act with the Federal Constitution, or when the conflict arises between infra-constitutional standards or acts which, 'within their hierarchical level, "indirectly" infringe on the federal Constitution which establishes the precedence of the higher standard or act over the lower ones'.

To the cases provided for in the three previously mentioned Clauses must be added two other cases, which were admitted in a praetorian way by the case law of the Supreme Court itself: the extraordinary appeals for arbitrary judgment and for institutional gravity, of which the former are the vast majority of the cases presented for decision by the Supreme Court.

The latter has led to serious problems in the Court's functioning because, in a way, it constitutes it as simply another judicial level, when its function should be that of the highest tribunal of constitutional guarantees and head of the judicial branch of the whole nation.

The topic is also linked with federalism because the absence of clear standards in the case law of the Court has enabled the review of questions previously passed to local or provincial justice.

For this reason, though we cannot go into the subject,[182] attempts have been made to speed up the functioning of the Supreme Court through two main measures: (a) the introduction of the writ of certiorari, through Article 280 of the national Code of Civil and Commercial Procedures, according to Law 23.774 of 1990, which authorizes the Supreme Court to use its discretion and purely invoke the norm to reject extraordinary reviews when they lack sufficient federal damage, or the issues presented lack substance or importance; and (b) establishing case law of the National Supreme Court, based on the 1986 *Strada* and 1988 *Di Mascio* cases, requiring that in all the processes dealt with before provincial courts and in which there is a federal issue, it should be the respective Provincial higher Tribunal or Supreme Court that has the obligation to decide the federal issue, prior to the intervention of the federal Supreme Court by extraordinary review.

§2. Guarantees of Judicial Independence

90. The magistrates enjoy a guarantee of independence for their work because they are immovable and keep their posts as long as they are of good conduct. They can be removed only for malpractice, grave negligence, delays in exercising their functions, inexcusable lack of knowledge of the law, alleged committing of offences or physical or psychological incapacity. They enjoy the same immunity from arrest as the legislators.

182. *See* Germán J. Bidart Campos (2000a & 2000b); Vanossi & Ubertone (1996).

They receive a monthly salary set by law for their services; the salary cannot be reduced by an act of authority or with discounts except for those that the authority sets for pension or benefit purposes.

The tenure and remuneration of federal judges is protected under Article 110, in the interests of securing judicial independence.

§3. Supreme Court of Justice: Appointment and Removal, Composition and Competences

91. The Supreme Court of Justice is established by Article 108 of the Constitution, but the number of its members is settled by law. Currently, the Court is composed of five Justices, called Ministers. They resolve and choose, each year, the President of the Court.

The nomination procedure conditions to a great extent the functional independence of those who are finally appointed and, consequently, their performance as members of the Judicial branch.[183] The subject involves the day-to-day effectiveness of the separation and balance of powers as distinctive elements of the republican principle of government. It should be noted that in our institutional system every magistrate has 'judicial power' and therefore exercises control of constitutionality.

The form of selecting and nominating those responsible for administering justice has been a topic of interest since ancient times. Aristotle, in his *Politics*, presented the elements on which the good legislator should meditate what is appropriate for each political regime, among which he mentioned the one 'who is in charge of the administration of justice';[184] he declared that the differentiation of this aspect in the various kinds of regimes is based on three factors: 'the people among whom they are formed, the matters on which they decide and the method by which they are named … '.[185]

In Argentina, appointments are made by the President, with the consent of the Senate, in public meeting. It is necessary to distinguish between appointments to the Supreme Court and to other lower federal judgeships. In the first case, the Constitution – Article 99, Clause 4 – requires the consent of two-thirds of present members of the Senate. The vast majority of justices of the Supreme Court come from the Federal Capital, and very few are drawn from the provinces.

183. We are talking about judicial independence in relation to the political powers, that is, the most usual meaning of the term. As political powers we mean only the executive and legislative (without ignoring the political function exercised by the judicial branch in some circumstances, as ultimate interpreter of the Constitution). For the purposes of this work, we are ignoring other assumptions of 'judicial dependence' presented by the doctrine, such as 'dependence on popular clamor or on the will of the majorities', 'dependence proper to the judicial structure' and 'dependence on internal bureaucracy'. *See* Gargarella (1996:231–232).

184. Book Four, Ch. XIV. Translated by Carlos García Gual & Aurelio Pérez Jiménez (Barcelona: Ediciones Altaya, 1997), 174.

185. Book Four, Ch. XVI, *ibid.*, 182. As is known, Book Four analyses the different kinds of political regimes, divided into normal – monarchy, aristocracy and republic – and abnormal – tyranny, oligarchy and democracy – respectively.

In the other case, the appointment is based on a short list of three candidates nominated by the Council of the Magistracy, and only the simple majority of votes of the present members of the Senate is required. In practice, however, the will of the President normally prevails.

Nevertheless, the goal of the establishment of the Council of the Magistracy was to diminish political influence over the judges. It is difficult to eliminate that influence in the appointments of the President and the consents of the Senate.

92. According to Article 111, to be a member of the Supreme Court it is necessary to be a lawyer of the nation, with eight years of practice, and with the same qualifications required to be a Senator.

93. Justices of the Supreme Court are removed by means of impeachment through the Congress. The House of Deputies has the power to impeach the justices of the Supreme Court before the Senate in cases that are brought against them for misconduct or crimes committed in the fulfilment of their duties; or for ordinary crimes, after their discovery and after the decision to bring an action has been voted by a majority of two-thirds of its members present.

94. As noted previously, the Supreme Court has original jurisdiction in some matters and has appellate jurisdiction over all matters falling within the federal judicial power, including the interpretation and application of the Constitution.

§4. Council of the Magistracy and Jury: Composition and Competences

95. In the 1994 Constitutional reform, the Council of the Magistracy was established with the goal of ensuring the independence of the judicial power.

According the law,[186] it is composed of thirteen members (six legislators, three judges, one academician, two lawyers and one representative of the executive branch). The President of the Council is appointed by absolute majority of the total of its members.

Its functions are as follows: (a) to nominate three candidates to the President for appointment, with legislative agreement, to lower federal courts; (b) to administer the budget of the courts; (c) to be responsible for disciplinary proceedings, deciding the opening of removal proceedings of judicial magistrates; and (d) to make the rules for judicial organization.

96. Magistrates in lower courts can be denounced by any member of the public before a jury for their simple destitution, based on the reasons justifying this. The Jury, created after 1994 reform by Article 115, is made up of members of the Legislative branch, Judges and lawyers.

186. Law 26.080 (2006).

The decision, which cannot be appealed, shall have no other effect than the removal of the accused. But the condemned party shall nevertheless be subject to accusation, trial and punishment according to law before the ordinary courts.

If no decision is taken after 180 days from the opening of the proceedings for removal, the proceedings are to be filed and the suspended judge shall be reinstated.

§5. The Public Ministry

97. The Public Ministry is an independent body with functional autonomy and financial autarky, with the function of promoting justice in defence of the legal character of the general interests of society, in coordination with the other authorities of the republic, as per Article 120 since the 1994 Constitutional Reform. It is composed of the Attorney General of the nation, a General Defender of the Nation and such other members as established by the law.[187]

187. Law 24.946 (1998).

Part III. The Federal State

Chapter 1. Form of State: Federalism[188]

98. Argentina is a federal state consisting of the Federal Government, twenty-four subnational governments (twenty-three Provinces and the Autonomous City of Buenos Aires, which is the Federal Capital) and approximately 2.150 local governments.

As in the case of the United States, fourteen historical Provinces created the federal state, delegating part of their powers to the Federal Government and keeping the residual ones. This is an integrative federalism, which differs from a devolutive federalism, in which the central government gives powers back to the subnational entities. New provinces later became part of the federation, and the 1994 Constitutional Reform created the Autonomous City of Buenos Aires as another member.

99. Throughout its history, Argentina has undergone a profound centralization process that has produced a severe dislocation between the formal Constitution and reality. This constitutes a blatant breach of the federal project of the Constitution, which forces us to reconsider federalism from a realistic or sociological point of view, pushing us to examine the real validity of its normative aspect.

§1. History of Argentine Federalism

100. Federalism is a process rather than a political stereotype, and we can see the following stages in its legislative development in Argentina:

- First stage: federalism in the original 1853 Constitution.[189]
- Second stage: federalism in the 1860 Constitutional Reform.[190]
- Third stage: towards a 'consensus' federalism (from 1950 onwards). During this stage, a trend from 'dual' or competitive federalism towards a 'cooperative' or 'consensus' federalism begins, since the powers of Article 107 of the 1853–1860 text (currently Article 125) have begun to be exercised: 'The provinces may enter

188. In relation to the Argentine federation, *see* Hernández (1997a; 2004b; 2005a; 2006a; and 2008a, Chs I, II and III and 2009b, Chs I, II, III, IV, V and VI).
189. *See* the General Introduction and Part I of this book.
190. *See ibid.*

into partial treaties for purposes of the administration of justice, of economic interests and works of common benefit, with the knowledge of Congress … .'

Thus, provincial pacts that had stopped being signed after 1853 shyly start to appear from 1948 onward, becoming firmer at the beginning of the 1950s and continuing to this day, with different purposes and denomination, allowing the construction of bridges and an interprovincial tunnel, the treatment of interprovincial rivers as a watershed unit, the creation of hydrology committees, the creation of the Federal Investments Council and other federal councils for diverse matters, as well as for the solving of problems and the analysis of projects.

– Fourth stage: the deepening of federalism in the 1994 Constitutional Reform. The Constitutional Reform of 1994, the result of the Federal Constitutional Convention that met in the cities of Santa Fe and Paraná during that year, had as one of its driving ideas the deepening of the decentralization of power in Argentina.

The debate over this issue[191] (in which we had the honour of participating as Vice President of the Drafting Committee) covered three main chapters: federalism, municipal autonomy, included in Article 123 of the Federal Constitution, and the autonomy of the City of Buenos Aires, which was recognized in its category of city-state (in our view), with an institutional standing very similar to that of the Provinces, according the current Article 129 of the Federal Constitution.[192]

In specific relation to federalism, this constitutional reform covered various aspects: (a) institutional and political, (b) financial and (c) economic and social.

101. In institutional and political terms, the constitutional reform established the following amendments:

(a) *Four levels of government in the Argentine federation.* In effect, there are currently these levels: the Federal Government (Article 44–120), provincial governments (Articles 121–128), government of the Autonomous City of Buenos Aires (Article 129) and municipal governments (Article 123), with their respective competences and autonomies, which express the decentralization of political power in the country. Hence, Argentine federal society is composed of the Federal Government, twenty-three provinces and the Autonomous City of Buenos Aires, now the seat of the Federal Capital. The Federal Government does not have direct relationships with the municipal governments because they work through provincial governments and states. The reform also included regions within the Constitution (Article 124), which are established as a union of provinces but only for economic and social development and not as new political entities.

191. *See* Hernández (1997a, 2004a and 2009b). In Hernández (2004b), there is a comparative study of institutions and powers in compound states. *See* our constitutional work in Hernández (1995a).

192. *See* our book 'La Ciudad Autónoma de Buenos Aires y el federalismo argentino', Jusbaires, Buenos Aires, 2017, before mentioned.

(b) *Distribution of competences.* The 1994 Constitutional Reform did not modify the Constitution in the fundamental matter of distribution of competences in the federal state, which is former Article 104 (currently Article 121), summarizing the historical Law of the Argentines.
(c) *The Senate and its federal role.* The reform produced these changes: (1) the inclusion of a third senator per province, corresponding to the second political party in elections, that is, the minority (Article 54); (2) the direct, instead of indirect, election of senators, and the reduction of their terms of office from nine years to six (Articles 54 and 56 amending prior Articles 46 and 48); and (3) greater stress on the federal role, making the Senate the originating organ for the debate of two fundamental laws: the law on tax sharing (Article 75, Clause 2) and the laws on harmonic development of the nation and the population of its territory and the promotion of differentiated policies to balance the unequal relative development of provinces and regions (Article 75, Clause 19).
(d) *Federal intervention.* We have had more than 170 interventions, of which two-thirds were decreed by the President of the republic and the remaining third by a Law of Congress. To avoid this abusive exercise of the institute that has been one of the causes of centralization of the country, the reform established that only Congress may declare the federal intervention of the Provinces or of the Autonomous City of Buenos Aires (Article 75, Clause 31) and that Congress can approve or revoke any intervention decreed by the President during the recess of Congress. In turn, Article 99, Clause 20, established that, if the Executive branch decrees an intervention during the recess of the Legislative branch, then it must simultaneously call for extraordinary sessions to discuss the measure.
(e) *Political parties and federalism.* Since political parties have been included in the Constitution in Article 38, with the obligation to respect the Constitution, they must accept the values and principles of federalism not only in the state organization but also in their own organization and functioning. One more reason for the country's de-federalization has been the non-compliance with these principles by the largest national political parties.

102. Regarding *fiscal federalism*, the constitutional reform set the following items:

(a) *Distribution of fiscal competences.* The reform updated the distribution of fiscal competences established in the original Constitution of 1853 for the Nation and Provinces, under the division in direct and indirect taxes.
(b) *Tax sharing.* The 1994 reform prescribes a tax sharing system between the federal and the provincial governments because it had existed by the creation of successive regulations since 1935.

In effect, Article 75, Clause 2, of the Federal Constitution currently reads as follows: 'An agreement-law based on understandings between the Nation and the provinces shall establish systems of joint participation for these taxes, guaranteeing the automatic remittance of funds.'

This agreement law must also comply with the following conditions according to the Supreme Law: (1) The Senate is the House of origin. (2) The enactment must be with the absolute majority of all the members of each House. (3) It cannot be amended unilaterally. (4) It cannot be regulated. (5) It must be approved by the provinces. (6) The distribution between the Federal Government, the Provinces and the City of Buenos Aires, and among these, shall be made in direct connection with the competences, services and functions of each of them, considering objective distribution criteria. (7) These criteria must be: equity, solidarity and a priority to achieve an equivalent degree of development, quality of life and equal opportunities in all the Argentine territory.

This agreement law is, for us, essential for supporting consensus federalism in one of the most conflictive areas of Argentine history: the financial relationship between the Federal Government and the Provinces. Unfortunately, the sixth Temporary Provision of the 1994 Constitutional Reform has not been complied with, which indicated a term for the enactment of the tax sharing agreement law 'prior to the end of 1996'.

The detailed criteria for sharing must be determined at the time of discussion about the primary distribution because many services have passed from the national to the provincial sphere and also to the municipal sphere in a decentralization process that we consider fundamental for the future of the country. Consequently, an increase in the percentage corresponding to the Provinces and to the City of Buenos Aires will be required, with parts to be given to the Municipalities.

(c) *Federal fiscal Body*. According to Article 75, Clause 2: 'A federal fiscal body shall be in charge of the control and monitoring of what is laid down in this paragraph, according to the law which shall guarantee the representation of all the provinces and of the City of Buenos Aires as regards its composition.' Thus, the Constitutional Convention gave the maximum hierarchy to a body called the Federal Tax Commission, which was created by Law 20.221 in 1971.

(d) *Budget federal principles*. This is another important amendment provided for by Article 75, Clause 8, which adds to the attribution of the Congress to fix the budget of the federation, the following formula: 'according to the standards laid down in the third paragraph of Clause 2 of this Article'.

We should remember that these standards are those indicated for the agreement law on the joint participation of taxes. That is, this paragraph contains a constitutional policy that associates the budget with essential issues of the federal project: the regionalization, integration, decentralization and strengthening of the autonomies of the Provinces, the Autonomous City of Buenos Aires and the Municipalities.

Unfortunately, these guidelines have not been observed either since the 1994 Constitutional Reform.

103. Economic and social aspects incorporated into the Federal Constitution in 1994 include the following:

(a) *The Federal Bank*: Article 75, Clause 6 prescribed that the Congress shall: 'establish and regulate a Federal bank with the power to issue money, as well as other national banks'. The text challenges the suitability of the current Central Bank, the creation and denomination of which are inherent to a unitarian rather than a federal state, and follows the examples of other federations such as those of the US or Germany.

(b) *Regions for economic and social development*: As indicated in Article 124: 'The provinces are empowered to create regions for the economic and social development and to establish entities with powers for the fulfillment of their purposes.'

This amendment is very important and means, in the first place, that the purpose of the region must be the promotion of economic and social development. In the second place, the region cannot consist of a new level of political government because in the Argentine federal structure, as we have seen, there are only four government levels. In the third place, the region has a state public legal status, limited to the promotion of the economic and social development, and the creation of which depends on the will of the provinces. In the fourth place, the region is a means to strengthen Argentine federalism[193] and, consequently, this instrument cannot be used to centralize the country or to harm provincial and municipal autonomies.[194]

Regions have been created by interprovincial pacts. Most of the Provinces are part of regions: Salta, Jujuy, Tucumán, Catamarca, Chaco, Formosa, Santiago del Estero, Misiones and Corrientes created the Norte Grande Region (1987); Mendoza, San Juan, San Luis and La Rioja created the Nuevo Cuyo Region (1988); La Pampa, Neuquén, Río Negro, Chubut, Santa Cruz and Tierra del Fuego created the Patagonia Region (1996); and Córdoba, Santa Fé and Entre Ríos created the Central Region (1998 and 1999). In our opinion, this is a very important characteristic of Argentine Federalism.

(c) *The provinces and international relations*: Article 124 of the Federal Constitution, after referring to the provincial powers to create regions, says:

> and they are also empowered, with the knowledge of the Congress, to enter into international agreements provided they are consistent with the national foreign policy and do not affect the powers delegated to the Federal Government or the public credit of the Nation. The City of Buenos Aires shall have the regime which is to be established to that effect.

The need for supranational integration, imposed by globalization, interdependence and acute economic world competition, has encouraged the development of binational border subregions involving some Argentine Provinces.

193. As anticipated by Zarza Mensaque (1977).
194. In a detailed study in Hernández (1997a and 2000), we present the amendments that must be put into practice in accordance with the constitutional reform and under the provisions of national and international integration.

Under the Mercosur, and as a consequence of the Protocols of Border Subregional Integration, Crecenea and Codesul were created, bringing together the Argentine Provinces and the States of South of Brazil with the purpose of promoting foreign trade and integration.

The members of the Constituent Convention distinguished these agreements from treaties because of their more limited scope.[195]

(d) *The provinces and the original ownership of natural resources.* The Federal Constitution, in the last paragraph of Article 124, expresses the following: 'The Provinces shall have the original dominion over the natural resources existing in their territory.'

This ownership includes the sea, hydrocarbons, energy, fishing, and so forth and presupposes the relevant amendments to legislation by Congress. In addition, for the exploration, exploitation and use of natural resources, with sustainable development, a very large field is opened up for consensus federalism by means of the use of interjurisdictional relationships and entities. Such institutional modernization will be an indispensable requirement to face the great challenge involved in transformation into a developed, integrated and balanced country.

(e) *Provincial social security entities.* Article 75, Clause 19 established the reaffirmation of the concurrent authority of the provinces to 'continue with their own social security entities for civil servants and professionals; and ... promote economic progress, human development, creation of jobs, education, science, knowledge and culture',[196] and the imposition on Congress of a requirement, in exercising its powers over education and culture, to respect local diversity and pluralism in various ways.

In conclusion, it is of utmost importance for the country to comply with the federal project of the Constitution. It is clear that this matter is intertwined with another complex problem: the lack of a political and juridical culture of respect for the Constitution.

---

195. Sagués (1994) declared that 'Provincial-international agreements may not exceed the provincial competences in their contents (for which reason they can only operate in issues relevant to the provinces or where these have powers concurrent with the Federal Government) and in addition, they have to respect the existing federal law (constitutional and infra-constitutional), prior and subsequent to the provincial-international agreement.'

As regards the limits to these agreements, the Constitution expressly mentions them in its text, but the analysis is not included here for the sake of brevity. *See* Hernández (1997a and 2009b).

196. *See* Art. 125, Clause 2 of the Constitution.

§2. THE DISTRIBUTION OF COMPETENCES[197]

104. On the fundamental topic of the distribution of competences in the federal state, the Constitutional Reform of 1994 did not modify the highest rule on this subject, the old Article 104 (current 121), originated in the Constitution of 1853. The concepts of Alberdi and Gorostiaga, that the Provinces have unrestricted residuary powers, and that the Federal Government exercises those expressly or implicitly delegated and therefore has limited powers, have full force, as accepted by the doctrine and case law of the Supreme Court.

It is true that this rule has undergone modifications, as the centralization process has evolved in the country, and even the case law of the Supreme Court itself has admitted the advances of the central government, as authors such as Vanossi, Frías, Bidart Campos, Romero and so on have noted, but we trust that the changes that have to take place in the future, in accordance with the constitutional mandate emerging from the reform, will deepen federalism.

105. The *classifications* made by the doctrine about the relations of the federal structure are, therefore, still in force. These relations, we remember, are of subordination (Articles 5 and 31, establishing the supremacy of the National Constitution), participation (of the Provinces and of the Autonomous City of Buenos Aires in the Federal Government, specifically in the Senate) and coordination (which is the delimitation of competences of the federal and provincial governments and that of the City of Buenos Aires), as mentioned by Germán Bidart Campos.[198]

Likewise, different classifications of competences between the Federal Government and the provinces are also in force, which we can summarize as follows: *conserved by the provinces* (Article 121); *delegated to the Federal Government* (fundamentally the express competences of the various Federal Government bodies, for example, Articles 75, 85, 86, 99, 100, 114, 115 and 116, and those implicit of the Congress, Article 75, Clause 32); *concurrent between government orders* (Articles 41 and 75, Clauses 2, 17, 18, 19, first paragraph, and Article 125); *shared* (requiring the will of the levels of government, such as the law agreement of tax sharing and the federal tax body, and the transfers of competences, services and functions, Article 75, Clause 2); and *exceptional* (for the Federal Government in direct taxes, Article 75, Clause 2, and for the provincial governments in dictating the underlying codes until these are dictated by Congress, and for arming warships or raising armies in cases of foreign invasion or of a danger so imminent that it admits no delay, Article 126).

There are also competences forbidden to the Provinces (because they were delegated to the Federal Government), forbidden to the Federal Government (because they were maintained by the Provinces) and forbidden to every order of government (such as the concession of extraordinary faculties, of the sum of public power

---

197. For this topic we follow our article 'The distribution of competences and the tendency toward centralization in the Argentine Federation', in 'Decentralizing an Re-centralizing trends in the distribution of powers within Federal Countries', 2008 Annual Meeting of the International Association of Centers for Federal Studies, held in Barcelona, published by the Institut d Estudis Autonomics, 2008, pp. 71 and ff. Also *see* Hernández (1997a, 2004b and 2009b).

198. *See* Bidart Campos (1972:120–121).

or submissions or supremacies to government or to any person, Article 29, or the violation of the declarations, rights and guarantees of the dogmatic part of the Supreme Law).

We have said that since the reform, the federal relationship is binding on the Federal Government, the twenty-three provinces and the Autonomous City of Buenos Aires, and in consequence the previously mentioned classifications are, in general, applicable. However, as the City of Buenos Aires has a special nature, that of city-state, distinguishing it from the Provinces and Municipalities, some special considerations must be made.[199]

106. The Constitutional Reform of 1994 *added* the following competences to the Federal Government:[200]

(1) to establish and modify specific allocations of shareable tax resources, for specific periods by special law (Article 75, Clause 3);
(2) to provide for the harmonious growth of the nation and for populating its territory; to promote differential policies in order to balance the unequal relative development of provinces and regions (Article 75, Clause 19);
(3) to sanction laws organizing and giving a basis for education, consolidating national unity, respecting provincial and local particularities, within compliance with particular requirements (Article 75, Clause 19);
(4) to approve or reject the new international treaties incorporated by the reform, that is, human rights treaties, with future constitutional hierarchy, integration treaties, standards set by supranational bodies and international treaties signed by the provinces (Article 75, Clauses 22 and 24, and Article 124);
(5) 'to legislate positive measures guaranteeing true equality of opportunities and treatment, and the full benefit and exercise of the rights recognized by this Constitution and by the international treaties on human rights in force' (Article 75, Clause 23);
(6) to dictate a special, comprehensive social security regime protecting children in situations of neglect and of the mother during pregnancy and the nursing period (Articles 75 and 23);
(7) to arrange or decree federal intervention (Article 75, Clause 31, and Article 99, Clause 20);
(8) to exercise the government function, the headship of which is recognized in the person of the President of the Nation (Article 99, Clause 1);
(9) to exercise the general administration of the country, through the head of the Cabinet, politically responsible to the President of the Nation, and under the control of the General Accounting Office of the Nation (Article 85, Clause 1, and 100, Clause 1);
(10) to dictate under particular conditions decrees of necessity and urgency except in penal, tax, electoral and political party matters (Article 99, Clause 3);

199. *See* Hernández (1997), Ch. IV.
200. Following the careful listing made by Castorina de Tarquini (1995:351–352).

(11) to organize the collection of the national revenue and to execute the national budget law, as a faculty of the head of the Cabinet, who exercises this under the supervision of the President of the nation (Article 99, Clause 10, and Article 100, Clause 7);
(12) to organize and administer justice. The selection of magistrates is now made by a special body, the Council of the Magistracy, which does not include provincial representation. The appointment is always made by the President with the agreement of the Senate (Article 99, Clause 4, and Article 114).

107. The constitutional reform also increased the exclusive competences of the Provinces:[201]

(1) to dictate the Provincial Constitutions in accordance with Article 5, ensuring municipal autonomy and regulating their scope and content in the institutional, political, administrative, economic and financial aspects (Article 123). This provision shows the levels of political decentralization, and thus the increasingly of Provincial Constitutions trend towards recognizing municipal autonomy;
(2) to create regions for economic and social development and to establish bodies for carrying out these purposes (Article 124);
(3) to sign international agreements under certain conditions (Article 124);
(4) to exercise all those powers that are implied in the concept of original provincial ownership of the resources existing in their territories (Article 124);
(5) to exercise powers of policing and to levy taxes on premises of national interest in the territory of the republic (Article 75, Clause 30).

108. In terms of *concurrent faculties*, the reform incorporated the following: indirect internal taxes (Article 75, Clause 2); attributions related to the indigenous peoples of Argentina (Articles 75, Clause 17); and the provisions in the new clause of progress or human development (Articles 75, Clause 19, first paragraph, and 125). Even though there is no exact correlation in the text of these two norms, we agree with Castorina de Tarquini[202] in the interpretation that all the matters mentioned in Article 75, Clause 19, first paragraph, require the concurrent action of the Provinces, and we also consider that the generic statement of Article 125 comprises what is most specific in that norm. Article 41 likewise recognizes the faculty of the Nation to dictate 'the minimum protection standards' on the environment, and in Article 75, Clause 19, the 'laws referring to the organization and basis' of education, but in our opinion the previous constitutional doctrine on the complex topic of the concurrency of faculties has not been modified, just as we held in the Constitutional Convention itself.[203] Article 125 also prescribes that 'the Provinces and the City of Buenos Aires may continue with their own social security entities for civil servants and professionals', which should be interpreted as a ratification of the concepts already determined by Article 14*bis*, in a special defence of the faculties of

201. As noted by the respected researcher, Castorina de Tarquini (1995:353).
202. Castorina de Tarquini (1995:355).
203. *See* Hernández (1995a:60).

the Provinces and of the City of Buenos Aires against the attacks of the central government, which aimed at transferring the pension funds by means of Fiscal Pacts and other pressure.

Finally, regarding Article 42, which provides for 'the necessary participation of consumer and user associations and of the interested Provinces in the control entities', and in 'conflict prevention and settlement' and the 'regulations for national public utilities', we also share the opinion of Castorina de Tarquini[204] that a faculty that is, in principle, national may become concurrent by the will of the Provinces interested in participating. We add that the fact that the Provinces can participate, as in this case, in national agencies, should be stressed as another feature of the deepening of federalism.

109. In relation to the *new shared competences* embodied in the reform, the same author[205] indicates:

> 1) the establishment of the contributions-sharing regime, which will be made by means of a law agreement, on the basis of accords between the Nation and the provinces … 2) In the same constitutional provision [referring to Article 75, Clause 2] another shared faculty is established when it is provided that there will be no transfers of competences, services or functions without the respective reallocation of resources, approved by Law of Congress as appropriate, and by the interested Province or the City of Buenos Aires. Such a transfer will thus operate as long as there is a willingness shared between the different orders of political power … 3) Finally, the control and monitoring of the tax-sharing and of any transfer of services will be the responsibility of a federal fiscal agency, with representation of all the Provinces and of the City of Buenos Aires, so that this function will also be exercised in a shared manner (Article 75, Clause 2).

To sum up, the most important federal competences correspond to the three powers of the state: legislative, executive and judicial, summarized in the management of common defence, of foreign relations and of the general interests of the country; and the most important subnational competences are those that have to do with the interests of each of the Provinces, through the conserved faculties, and the Autonomous City of Buenos Aires, and, in general, with the competences that enable local autonomy in its constitutional, political, financial and local administrative aspects.

It is our opinion that there has been an extensive interpretation of the federal competences, which has permitted a sharp process of centralization in the country.

110. Another important aspect to consider is that of the *intergovernmental relations* in our federation. Article 107, sanctioned with the original Constitution of 1853–1860 and maintained in the Constitutional Reform of 1994 in the current Article 125, provides for 'domestic' treaties between the Provinces. This norm, as

204. Castorina de Tarquini (1995:358).
205. *Ibid.*, (1995:359–360).

from the 1950s, made possible the transition from a dual or competitive federalism to one that is cooperative or consensus federalism.

Likewise, progress was made towards greater interjurisdictional relations through federal councils, which include the joint participation of representatives of the federal and provincial governments.[206] This, naturally, was an indication of a road of flexibilization in the use of the competences and institutional practices. But, we must repeat, this is a matter of a process under way, which must be reaffirmed.

At present, for the political and institutional circumstances we are experiencing, we are far from putting into practice the important modifications that have to be made in our public law, to deepen the decentralization of power and integration, as the appropriate responses of our Constitution to the challenges of the globalized world in which we live.

As for the possibility of *international integration*, the Constitutional Reform of 1994 in its Article 75, Clause 24 has provided, as a faculty of the National Congress:

> To approve treaties of integration which delegate powers and jurisdiction to supranational organizations under reciprocal and equal conditions, and which respect the democratic order and human rights. The rules derived therefrom have a higher hierarchy than laws. The approval of these treaties with Latin American States shall require the absolute majority of all the members of each House. In the case of treaties with other States, the national Congress, with the absolute majority of the members present of each House, shall declare the advisability of the approval of the treaty, which shall only be approved with the vote of the absolute majority of all the members of each House, one hundred and twenty days after said declaration of advisability. The denouncement of treaties referred to in this sub-section shall require the prior approval of the absolute majority of all the members of each House.

As a consequence, this possibility of supranational integration has been constitutionalized, in accordance with the times in which we live.

Argentina is part of a regional system, the OAS (Organization of American States), with a system of protecting human rights based on the American Declaration of the Rights and Duties of Man and on the American Convention on Human Rights (Pact of San José de Costa Rica, 1969).

The American Convention, in section 28 dealing with the *federal clause*, declares:

> (1) Where a State Party is constituted as a federal state, the national government of such State Party shall implement all the provisions of the Convention over whose subject matter it exercises legislative and judicial jurisdiction.
> (2) With respect to the provisions over whose subject matter the constituent units of the federal state have jurisdiction, the national government shall immediately take suitable measures, in accordance with its constitution and its laws,

206. Such as the Federal Investments Council, the Federal Taxes Council and the Federal Councils on Education, Health, the Environment, Public Works, Domestic Security, etc.

to the end that the competent authorities of the constituent units may adopt appropriate provisions for the fulfillment of this Convention.

(3) Whenever two or more State Parties agree to form a federation or other type of association, they shall take care that the resulting federal or other compact contains the provisions necessary for continuing and rendering effective the standards of this Convention in the new state that is organized.

In consequence, the Argentine Provincial States must adapt their legislation and judicial case law to the American Convention, in the same way that the Federal Government must scrupulously respect the federal principles of the Constitution in this supranational integration process, taking care not to affect the provincial and municipal competences and autonomies. Likewise, as we have said before, there must also be participation of the Provinces and Municipalities both in the ascendant and in the descendant phase of international integration treaties.[207]

The fact is that this is a process under way, in which we are very far from integration processes such as those of the European Union.

As we saw earlier, according to the Constitutional Reform of 1994, Article 124, the Provinces also have faculties to sign 'international agreements', with the limitations expressed therein. This has also meant a fundamental modification that indicates the road to follow in the globalized world of which we are part.

§3. The Trend to Centralization

111. Throughout the history of Argentina, we have undergone a profound centralization process, which has produced notable discordance between the normative Constitution and the current reality. This forces us to consider federalism in its *sociological or realist face*, aiming to observe the genuine currency of the constitutional norms.

A multiplicity of reasons has led to the failure to comply with the federal project of the Constitution, which Frías has summarized as:

(a) the advance of the Federal Government without sufficient resistance from the provinces (as in tax matters or in federal interventions);
(b) the development of centralizing virtualities of the Constitution itself (such as from the legislative faculties of the Congress or the commercial clause); and
(c) the infrastructure of socioeconomic concentration in the Metropolitan Area of Buenos Aires to the detriment of the interior and of the equilibrium of the country.[208]

207. *See* Hernández (2000).
208. *See* Frías (1985:389).

We added these causes of centralization:[209] *(1) The coup d'état,* that we suffered in our history, in 1930, 1943, 1955, 1962, 1966 and the last one in 1976, which meant the breaking of the Constitution and the republican and federal principles, and the lack of autonomy of Provinces and Municipalities. (2) The *emergencies*, in different political, economical and social orders, with particular influence in the centralization of powers in the Federal level of government, and, specially in the hands of the Presidency. And (3) The *'hyperpresidentialism'*, which meant the advance of the Presidency over the other Branches of Government, without adequate political control from the Congress, and practically without judicial review from the Judiciary. And this pathology not only affected republican principles but also federalism as form of State and government.

We have sustained that the Argentine's declination began with the 1930 coup d'état, and it is possible to observe this phenomenon in different aspects. For instance, Professor Alberto Porto[210] showed that while in 1922 the Argentine gross product represented the 51.8% of the all South American Countries, now we only reached the 11.4%.

It is important to notice that the centralization process was an historical trend, but it was deepened from 1930. But when the *democracy was restored in 1983*, we had a transcendent exercise of the Provincial and Municipal autonomies, which meant the modernization of our State Constitutionalism and Local Governments. Furthermore, this process was the direct antecedent of the National Constitutional Reform of 1994, where the same goal was achieved at the federal level. However, we continue with the violations of the Constitutions and the Laws, as we see later in the point of Constitutional and legal culture.

On the violations of the Constitution, we repeat the following ideas contained in an article that we titled 'The failure of the centralist project':[211]

> The recent reports at the end of 2002 on human development from the United Nations and from the Institute of Research of the Cordoba Stock Exchange, have coincided on their diagnosis of the grave problems of inequality, injustice, inequity and disintegration, caused among other things by the extreme centralization of the country. It is sufficient for this to look at the human development indices contained in the first of these Reports, where in the case of Formosa as the lowest point they reach 0.156, and in the case of the city of Buenos Aires as the highest point, they reach 0.867, that is, almost 6 times more, as a demonstration of the territorial differences.
>
> The dangers and evils that have been pointed out since the 19th century by, among others, Alberdi in his 'Bases' opposing the capitalization of Buenos Aires, Sarmiento in 'Argirópolis' and Alem in his famous prophecy of 1880 in the debate on the federalization of the city of Buenos Aires. And in the 20th

209. *See* Antonio María Hernández, 'Fortalezas y debilidades constitutionales. Una lectura crítica en el Bicentenario', Abeledo Perrot, Buenos Aires, 2012, and 'Las emergencias y el orden constitucional', Instituto de Investigaciones Jurídicas de la Universidad Nacional Autónoma de Mexico, Mexico, 2003.

210. Alberto Porto, 'La enigmática evolución de la equivalencia económica argentino-sudameicana. De los datos de Bunge (1922/23 y 1937/38) a los actuales', www.blogeconosp.econo.unlp.edu.ar/wp/.

211. Published in *La Nación* newspaper of Buenos Aires, 8 Jan. 2003.

century, Martínez Estrada spoke to us of the 'head of Goliath' and more recently Félix Luna in his book 'Buenos Aires y el país' held that this is an unresolved structural problem that runs through all our history.

This notable phenomenon of concentration, which encompasses all the orders of Argentine social life in relation to its capital and is repeated in nearly all the provinces, has been similar to that occurring in other Latin American countries, which have unfortunately not been able to escape from this characteristic of underdeveloped societies, presenting poor territorial order, with marked asymmetries.

The centralization process of the country around its metropolitan area of Buenos Aires, where in less than 1% of the territory live nearly 35% of the population, is complemented by the circumstance that nearly 80% of Argentine produc tion originates in a radius that is hardly more than 500 km from that area.

It is clear to us that the federalism as a form of State embodied in the National Constitution of 1853 and 1860 was the correct decision for solving the grave political, economic and social problems of such an extensive country, which required an effective decentralization of power.

But the problematic currency of the Constitution could also be particularly seen in this aspect, since in reality a unitarizing project steadily imposed itself, centralizing power in the so-called Federal Government, based in the port of Buenos Aires, which encroached on the constitutional designs and on provincial autonomies, without respecting municipal autonomies either.

This negative process could not be hindered even by the constitutional reform of 1994, one of the main ideas of which was the deepening of the decentralization of power.

We can see that the *centralist project* has deepened in recent times, until 2015 mainly, affecting federal principles, as in the following areas.

I. Agreement Law on Tax Sharing

112. It should be noted that the modification of the system of Law 23.548, sanctioned in 1988 during the presidency of Alfonsín, was started during the government of President Menem and his Minister Cavallo, in the 1990s, frequently through the use of decrees of necessity and urgency, and with the Fiscal Pacts, with the aim of reducing the percentage that had been recognized for the Provinces, and this was continued by the succeeding national governments.

In consequence, the centralist advance of the 'Federal' Government over the tax resources of the provinces and municipalities has been exacerbated, strengthening the economic, political and social dependence of these levels of government.

In effect, to the deductions made to primary distribution through the use of specific allocations, which began in the government of Dr Menem,[212] have been added the check tax and, especially, the retentions on the export of soybeans, corn and wheat. Thus, the guarantee fixed for the provinces by Articles 7 of Law 23.548, of receiving 34% as a minimum of the national tax income, including both shareable and other taxes, has also been violated, at huge damage to the other orders of government.

We believe it is essential to establish a national forum or conference of Governors, as are found in other federations such as Mexico or US, in order to consolidate interjurisdictional relationships and achieve a more balanced communication of the provinces in the face of the hegemonic power of the central government.

There must be no delay in sanctioning the tax sharing law agreement to put an end to the violation of the Constitution, which set a deadline that expired long ago, and because it is essential to change the depressing reality of Argentine federalism.

To escape from the present labyrinth of tax sharing, we must follow our Ariadne's thread, which is nothing more than respecting the mandates of the Constitution. A shareable amount must be set that is not reduced by the huge number of specific allocations current today, most or all of which must be derogated. Then primary and secondary distributions must be assigned on the basis of constitutional criteria. For this, it is decisive to emphasize the modifications of the competences, services and functions between the Nation, the Provinces and the City of Buenos Aires.

A greater recognition of the participation of the Provinces and the City of Buenos Aires, which necessarily will then have repercussions in the tax sharing with the Municipalities, will make later discussion on secondary distribution, where disputes arise between the larger, developed Provinces and the smaller, more backward ones, relatively simpler. It is here that what I have called the triumph of the centralist project has resulted in a country with enormous differences and imbalances, according to the indices of human development, gross product or income per capita, which it is time to modify. The solidarity criteria demanded by the Constitution must be respected, as other federations do, such as Canada, Australia or Germany, which are outstanding examples to be considered.

This complex and decisive debate must start now, following the established constitutional bases.[213] For this to happen, a truly overarching policy must be exercised that overcomes party antagonisms, strengthens interjurisdictional relationships and enables a balanced development of the country in accordance with the federal project of the Constitution.

---

212. *See* Hernández (1997), Ch. II, in which we have described that process, analysing the topic of tax-sharing, with an estimate of the huge amounts taken from the provinces and hence from the municipalities.

213. To contribute to this long-delayed and fundamental debate, the Institute of Federalism of the National Academy of Law and Social Sciences which I direct has published the book *Aspectos fiscales y económicos del federalismo argentino* (Córdoba, 2008), with contributions from economists, jurists and specialists in other disciplines.

II. Destination of Federal Public Spending

113. We consider that Article 75, Clause 8 is not being complied with, which establishes that the general expenditure budget of the nation must be set annually 'according to the standards laid down in the third paragraph of Clauses 2 of this Article', that is, those referring to the tax sharing law, in terms of objectivity, equity and solidarity. In consequence, the current situation of suffocating centralization that prevents the harmonious development of the country is not being modified.[214]

III. Lack of Progress in the Regional Integration Process

114. Even though the map of the regions is almost formalized with the already constituted regions of North Argentina, Patagonia, New Cuyo and Central, with only the lack of integration of the Province of Buenos Aires and the Autonomous City of Buenos Aires, no advance can be seen in the integration process. The institutional, economic and social situations being experienced, plus the absence of an overarching policy, have surely influenced this lack of progress. Some noteworthy activity has recently been seen only in the Central Region. The modification of territorial organization is urgent and includes strategic projects such as creating the bi-oceanic corridors, which involve carrying out significant infrastructure works such as the consolidation of the passes over the Andean Cordillera, in accordance with the agreement signed by the Mercosur with Chile.

IV. Lack of Compliance with Other Norms Related to Economic Aspects of Federalism

115. Here we include the lack of creation of the Federal bank, the maintenance of centralizing legislation that is not adapted to the principle of the Provinces' ownership of natural resources and the insufficient exercise of the new competences in international agreements that enable supranational integration, with the participation of Provinces and Municipalities.

V. Lack of 'Full' Autonomy for the Autonomous City of Buenos Aires

116. This brief analysis of the problems of Argentine federalism cannot omit what occurred with Article 129 of the National Constitution, which recognized full autonomy for the City of Buenos Aires, in one of the most significant advances of the Constitutional Reform of 1994. It is well known that the National Congress sanctioned Laws 24.588 and 24.620, which violated the letter and the spirit of this Constitution, restricting the autonomy of the City, by preventing it from having a police force and from its complete administration of justice. We commented on this

214. *See* the article 'Sin respeto por el federalismo', which we published in *La Nación* newspaper of Buenos Aires, 18 Dec. 2006.

situation,[215] which particularly affected our form of state and the Argentine Provinces, since they continue contributing to the national treasury that carries responsibility for the police and national justice service (civil, penal, commercial and labour matters) of the richest city in the country.

It is clear to us that the Constitution was not being complied with, in terms of our federal form of state, as is seen in relation to our republican form of government, particularly through the phenomenon of hyperpresidentialism. The decay in our rule of law implied the violation of the principles of the federal republic and an advance of the national government over the competences of the Provinces.

117. As a consequence of the election of new federal and provincial governments in 2015, it has begun the exercise of a *Cooperative Federalism* that has already achieved important agreements between the Federal Government and the Governors.

One example was the agreement around the return of 15% from the federal co-participatory mass to all the Provinces, according to the favourable ruling of the Supreme Court of Justice for the claim of the Provinces of San Luis, Santa Fe and Córdoba against the federal state.[216]

Another example was the agreement between the Federal Government and the Autonomous City of Buenos Aires was the transference of one part of the Federal Police to the Autonomous City of Buenos Aires, as we mentioned before.[217]

Special outline must be made on the Agreement reached on 16 November, 2017, between the President, the Governors, with the sole exception of the Province of San Luis, and the Head of Government of the Autonomous City of Buenos Aires, on very important and interjurisdictional matters. This Agreement has to be approved by Laws of Congress and the respective Legislatures of the Provinces and the Autonomous City of Buenos Aires, for its validity.

In consequence, the Congress enacted two Laws on 21 December, 2017: the Law No. 27,429, entitled Fiscal Consensus, which signified tax and social security modifications and was accompanied by the abandonment of the trials that the Provinces had initiated against the National State for the tax co-participation system, before the Supreme Court of Justice.[218]

And the other, No. 27,428, of Fiscal Responsibility and Good Government Practices, which established rules to guarantee solvency in national and provincial public accounts, avoiding excess expenses and the increase in the designation of public employees.

---

215. In the article titled 'La Ciudad de Buenos Aires y su autonomía plena', published in *La Nación* newspaper of Buenos Aires, 25 May 2007.

216. *See* Antonio María Hernández, 'Los fallos de la CSJN sobre detracciones a la masa coparticipable y la confirmación de una jurisprudencia federalista', Suplemento La Ley, Constitucional, Directora María Angélica Gelli, Buenos Aires, Abril 2016, Nº 2, pp. 44 y ff.

217. *See* Antonio María Hernández, 'La Ciudad Autónoma de Buenos Aires y el fortalecimiento del federalismo argentino', obr. cit.

218. In the Annex of the Agreement there is a list of the 59 Trials between both Governments.

On the other hand, local governments did not participate in the Agreement, but with adequate respect for their autonomy, in Article 33 it is proposed to the Provinces that they have to invite the local governments to adhere to the Law 27.428. Only in this way these obligations may be valid at that government level.

However, we must point out that these Agreements did not clearly specify the part of the co-participable funds that had to reach the Municipal Governments, which has led to conflicts between these governments and the provincial authorities, as observed in some cases.[219]

The Agreement also established a compensation to the Province of Buenos Aires for the co-participation funds for the Metropolitan Area of Buenos Aires.

These instruments, facts, dialogues and agreements between the Federal Government, Provinces and the Autonomous City of Buenos Aires were positive as exercise of cooperative federalism, but it is necessary more changes and overarching policy to comply the federal project of the Constitution.[220]

118. In this regard, we presented our twenty Proposals to strengthen Argentine federalism. In order to shorten this work, we only enumerate our Proposals:[221]

(1) Fulfil the principles of the republican and federal system of the National Constitution.
(2) End hyperpresidentialism.
(3) Strengthen the role of Congress and the Senate, in particular.
(4) Reaffirm the role of the Supreme Court of Justice of the Nation as guarantor of federalism.
(5) Promote a new territorial order of the country that modifies the enormous concentration of political, economic, demographic and cultural power in the Metropolitan Area of Buenos Aires.
(6) Sanction the tax co-participation agreement law, in accordance with the constitutional principles.
(7) Respect the federal principles in the annual sanction of the budgets.
(8) Federalize the Central Bank.
(9) Strengthen the federalism of coordination or agreement through a better exercise of the interjurisdictional relations. Creation of a National Association or Conference of Governors.
(10) Carry out a federal planning for the development of the country with the participation of the different levels.
(11) Promote regions for the economic and social development.
(12) Promote the new role of Regions, Provinces and Municipalities in the national and supranational integration processes.

---

219. Like in the Province of Cordoba, because the Constitution of the Province set forth in Art. 188, Clause 3 that not less than 20% of the Provincial Co-participation – including all kind of taxes: federal or provincial – correspond to the Local Governments.

220. In particular, it is urgent the enactment of the Tax Co-participation agreement Law, according the Constitution, which was specially mentioned in Clause m of the Agreement of 16 Nov. 2017.

221. For the exposition of the Proposals, *see* Antonio María Hernández, 'La Ciudad Autónoma de Buenos Aires y el fortalecimiento del federalismo argentino', obr. cit., pp. 85 and ff.

(13) Strengthen autonomy of the Provinces, the Autonomous City of Buenos Aires and the Municipalities.
(14) Modify or repeal the current centralist legislation and the respective policies.
(15) Federalize the education.
(16) Exercise a federalism of cooperation for the exploration, exploitation and use of natural resources.
(17) Federalize public services of national competence, in accordance with Article 42 of the Supreme Law.
(18) Strengthen federal principles in the doctrine and organization of the political parties.
(19) Decentralize and integrate the country in other aspects as infrastructure, communications and transport.
(20) Move the Federal Capital from the City of Buenos Aires.

Chapter 2. Subnational Institutions[222]

§1. Provinces

119. The autonomy of each Province or provincial state is acknowledged and includes institutional, political, financial and administrative aspects of each. This may be inferred from Article 122 of the Federal Constitution, which, when referring to the Provinces, states the following: 'They determine their own local institutions and are governed by them. They elect their governors, legislators, and other provincial officers, without the intervention of the Federal Government.'

The exercise of their constituent power is set forth in Article 5 of the Federal Constitution, which reads as follows:

> Each province shall enact its own Constitution under the republican, representative system, in accordance with the principles, declarations and guarantees of the National Constitution, ensuring its administration of justice, municipal regime, and elementary education. Under these conditions, the Federal Government shall guarantee each province the full exercise of its institutions.

In addition, the Constitution orders the following in Article 123: 'Each province enacts its own Constitution as stated in Article 5, ensuring municipal autonomy and ruling its scope and content regarding the institutional, political, administrative, economic and financial aspects.'

Consequently, the Provinces have enacted their Provincial Constitutions, first in an original manner, immediately after the enactment of the Federal Constitution, and second through the exercise of the derived constituent powers, when amending such Constitutions.

When enacting their constitutions, the Provinces must respect the basis of the previously mentioned Article 5, as well as the federal supremacy principle set forth in Articles 31 of the Federal Constitution, according to which:

> This Constitution, the laws of the Nation enacted by Congress in pursuance thereof, and treaties with foreign powers are the supreme law of the Nation; and the authorities of each province are bound thereby, notwithstanding any provision to the contrary included in the provincial laws or constitutions.

The federal Supreme Court of Justice is in charge of controlling the constitutionality of a Provincial Constitution, and it must assure the supremacy of the Federal Constitution.

In addition, in certain cases in which a province breaches the constitutional provisions of Article 5, the Federal Constitution also enables a federal intervention according to the provisions of Article 6, which grants the Federal Government the power to intervene in the provincial territory to secure a republican government,

---

222. For further information, *see* Hernández (2005a and 2009b).

among other grounds. This is a political intervention of an extraordinary nature, in order to assure the principles of the Argentine federation.

All the Provinces and the Autonomous City of Buenos Aires established republican systems of branch divisions: legislative, executive and judicial, as in the federal sphere. They are also presidential systems, with Governors in charge of the Executive branch and Legislatures in charge of the Legislative branch, all of whom are elected by the people.

Under the provincial autonomy acknowledged in Article 5 of the Federal Constitution, there are fifteen Provinces with unicameral systems and eight with bicameral systems. In general, the smaller and unpopulated Provinces adopted the first system, except for Córdoba, which adopted it with the 2001 Constitutional Reform. The larger and more populated Provinces have bicameral legislatures. The House of Representatives represents the people of the Province and the Senate represents the districts.

In the same manner as the Legislative branch, the Provinces differ in some aspects in the organization, appointment and functioning of the Judicial branch.

The Provincial Constitutions are the Supreme Laws of each of the Provinces and, consequently, acknowledge the main rights of citizens, organize the powers and establish the bases of the municipal regimes. They have a significant place and hierarchy in the federal constitutional scheme of the country. In general, they are more extensive and detailed than the Federal Constitution because they regulate the rights, provincial competences and the regimen of local governments.

§2. THE AUTONOMOUS CITY OF BUENOS AIRES

120. The Autonomous City of Buenos Aires, which is still the Federal Capital of the country, has a special status deriving from Article 129 of the Federal Constitution, which reads as follows:

> The City of Buenos Aires shall have an autonomous system of government with power of legislation and jurisdiction, and the Head of its government shall be directly elected by the people of the City. While the City of Buenos Aires is the Capital City of the Nation, a law shall guarantee the interests of the National State. According to the aforementioned provisions of this Article, the National Congress shall convoke the inhabitants of the City of Buenos Aires so that the representatives that are to be elected for that purpose issue the Organizing Statute of their institutions.

The Autonomous City of Buenos Aires is represented both in the House of Representatives and the Senate. With respect to its nature, in the discussion during the 1994 Constitutional Convention, we argued that it is a city-state, such as the cities of Berlin, Bremen and Hamburg in the German federation.[223]

223. *See* Hernández (1995a, 1997a and 2009b, Ch. V).

§3. Local Governments[224]

121. The municipal regime was included in the historical Constitution of 1853 in Article 5 as one of the requirements that Provinces have to ensure when enacting their Provincial Constitutions. After extensive discussion on its legal nature, the 1994 Constitutional Reform included in Article 123 the acknowledgment of municipal autonomy in these terms: 'Each province enacts its own Constitution as stated in Article 5, ensuring municipal autonomy and ruling its scope and content regarding the institutional, political, administrative, economic and financial aspects.'

The provinces must regulate their scope and content by means of their respective Provincial Constitutions and based on the following aspects: (a) institutional, which means the possibility of enacting the municipal charter (carta orgánica municipal), which is actually a local constitution; (b) political, which means the popular election of local authorities; (c) administrative, that is, the provision of utilities and other services that do not depend on any other government level; and (d) economic and financial, which means the free collection and investment of local income.

All Argentine Municipalities are autonomous, but there is a difference between those having 'total' autonomy, with the possibility of enacting their own charters, and those with 'partial' autonomy, lacking the institutional aspect. At present in Argentina there are more than 150 municipal charters enacted.

The Provinces are obliged to determine the basis for the local regimes, by virtue of the provisions of Articles 5 and 123 of the Federal Constitution. But they may only establish an 'autonomous' municipal regime, ensuring the previously mentioned aspects. Otherwise, the Federal Government may intervene in the Provinces if they do not respect the bases set forth in the Supreme Law.

Consequently, the relationships between the Federal Government and the municipalities are not direct but indirect, through the government of the Province where each municipality is located. Anyway, it is evident that the Federal Government is able to influence local life through its great political, economic and financial power.

In Argentina, there are no intermediate local entities between the municipalities and the provincial governments. But there is a growing development of the idea of 'intermunicipal relationships', which means the creation of several associative figures with different goals of common welfare, such as associations of municipalities, or intermunicipal entities, or production brokers or metropolitan entities. These do not exist in all of the Argentine territory but only in some Provinces. Such entities are created by the Municipalities, without the intervention of the provincial government, and the appointment of their authorities is the result of the decision of the respective Municipalities, represented there through their officers (in particular Mayors). Thus, there is no popular election for the conduction of such intermunicipal entities.

The municipal competences are fixed in each Provincial Constitution, in the Municipal Organic Law of each Province and in the respective Municipal Charters in the Municipalities that have enacted them. Municipal competence is quite broad because, in general, it reaches all matters related to the satisfaction of the common

---

224. For a detailed analysis, *see* Hernández (1997a), (1997b) and (2003b).

welfare needs of the local society. Such competences include the institutional, political, administrative, economic and financial aspects. Municipalities have their own powers, concurrent with those of the provincial and Federal Governments, and they also exercise some powers by delegation of such governments.

There are different systems for the allocation of competences, but in general the most common in our legal system is that which declares such powers in the Provincial Constitution and then, in a final clause, acknowledges the competences required to satisfy the needs of the local society.

The provincial constitutional provisions in general authorize the exercise not only of intermunicipal but also of interjurisdictional relationships, which provides a way to follow in the construction of a cooperative or consensus federalism, in which local governments must interrelate more and more with the other governmental levels. Nevertheless, there is much to be done in this matter.

Part IV. Protection of Fundamental Rights

Chapter 1. Fundamental Rights and Liberties

§1. The National and International Sources of Rights

122. The first Part of the Argentine Constitution, which is the system of values and beliefs, comes from the acknowledgment of various human rights and liberties, which are prior and superior to the State. The Federal Constitution calls this Part: 'Declarations, Rights and Guarantees'.

As we pointed out previously, the Constitutional Reform of 1994 incorporated international law on human rights; therefore, fundamental rights have a double source in Argentine constitutionalism: national and international. The former is divided in turn between the various levels of government: federal, provincial, of the Autonomous City of Buenos Aires and municipal because all of these exercise constituent power (although of varying degree) and have sanctioned their respective constitutions recognizing these rights.[225]

123. Rights are recognized in the National Constitution in the following norms: Articles 14, 20, 14*bis*, 15, 16, 9 to 12, 26, 17, 7, 8, 19, 28, 33, 36, 37, 38, 39, 40, 41, 42, 75 (Clauses 17, 19, 22, 23 and 24), 43, 18 and 125.

After noting the density of the rights, values and principles of the Constitution, it can be said that there is feedback between the dogmatic and organic parts[226] of the Constitution as well as of the Preamble and the Temporary Provisions.

There are principles that have constitutional roots such as the 'pro homine' (in favour of the person, so that the most favourable standard is chosen when national and international sources are used), the 'pro actione' (in favour of the action, so that the Judges using criteria of guarantees indicate to the defendant the best means to obtain effective legal protection) and the 'favour debilis' (so that the inferiority of conditions of the weaker part in a dispute are considered).

225. In the municipal case, it is worth clarifying that the scope of the fundamental rights recognized is more limited, because it refers especially to political and neighbourhood rights, as there is little sense making another recognition of other kinds of rights, already guaranteed by the other constitutions. *See* Hernández (2003b).

226. Because in the Constitutional Reform of 1994, the modification of the first thirty-five Articles of the Constitution was not permitted, and in consequence, new fundamental rights were incorporated in a new Chapter in this First Part, comprising Arts 36–43, and also in the Second Part, especially in Art. 75 on powers and duties of the Congress, in various Clauses, as we mentioned before.

The Provinces and the Autonomous City of Buenos Aires, exercising their constituent powers when enacting their respective Constitutions, include declarations of rights and guarantees in their dogmatic parts. In most cases, through applying Article 5 of the National Constitution, which provides for the currency of individual rights and guarantees in the Provinces, the statements of the National Constitution are repeated, which, by the way, is unnecessary.

Nonetheless, in the Provincial Constitutions a notable development of rights and guarantees can be seen, showing the wealth of the provincial public law (Hernández, 2008b). However, many of these norms do not have full and sufficient force in reality (*see* Hernández, Zovatto & Mora y Araujo, 2005b). They are 'offerings' that the constituent members made to the people, implying a commitment to produce the change for which the societies call. We have noted that there is not sufficient compliance with the law in Argentina, resulting from cultural underdevelopment in legal, political and democratic affairs. The emergencies of every kind, institutional, political, economic and social, have contributed to harming the rule of law, the republican system and the full force of individual rights and guarantees (Hernández, 2003a).

§2. Civil and Political Rights

124. The Constitution shows a common personalist and humanist philosophy in terms of civil and personal rights for its breadth and depth in its recognition of human rights. This is expressed in its indication that 'all the inhabitants' or 'all persons' enjoy the rights that prevent any discrimination (Articles 14, 16, 17, 18 and 43, for instance).

Rights and guarantees are recognized that protect civil liberty: conscience; physical integrity; defence in trial; correspondence and private papers; communications; the exercise of job or profession and so on; equality; freedom of religion, of expression, of the right to meet, of petition, of association, of teaching and learning and of property, among other rights proper to classical constitutionalism.

Among personal rights are those listed in Article 14:

> All the inhabitants of the Nation are entitled to the following rights, in accordance with the laws that regulate their exercise, namely: to work and perform any lawful industry; to navigate and trade; to petition the authorities; to enter, remain in, travel through, and leave the Argentine territory; to publish their ideas through the press without previous censorship; to make use and dispose of their property; to associate for useful purposes; to profess freely their religion; to teach and to learn.

In Article 33 of the National Constitution, non-enumerated rights are recognized: 'The declarations, rights and guarantees which the Constitution enumerates shall not be construed as a denial of other rights and guarantees not enumerated, but rising from the principle of sovereignty of the people and from the republican form of government.'

125. In terms of political rights, after 1994, the National Constitution makes an express democratic profession of faith and declares in Article 37 that: 'This Constitution guarantees the full exercise of political rights, in accordance with the principle of popular sovereignty and with the laws derived therefrom.'

In addition, according to Article 36: 'All citizens shall have the right to oppose resistance to those committing the acts of force' against constitutional order.'

The characteristics of suffrage are established in Article 37: 'Suffrage shall be universal, equal, secret and compulsory.'

The exercise of the institutes of direct or semidirect democracy is admitted, such as the popular consultation and the initiative. The political parties are constitutionalized, as fundamental instruments of the democratic system (*see* Part II, Chapter I).

Norms are incorporated regulating positive gender-oriented actions to guarantee the entry of women into elective public bodies. Article 37 of the National Constitution, incorporated in the Constitutional Reform of 1994, declares that real equality of opportunities between men and women for access to elective and party posts will be guaranteed by positive actions in the regulation of political parties and in the electoral regime. The 1927 Constitution of the Province of San Juan had recognized the right of women to vote, which showed a remarkably advanced provincial constitutionalism on the subject.[227] Political rights of women were recognized at the federal level in Argentina only from 1947 with the passing of Law 13.010 on female suffrage.[228]

§3. Economic, Social and Cultural Rights

126. As we said before, social constitutionalism means the recognition of social rights, also called 'second-generation' rights and the search for a 'welfare state'. The Constitution recognizes this class of rights in Article 14*bis*.

The social rights declared are related to the protection of the family, the rights of workers and especially as follows: (1) dignified and equitable conditions for carrying out their activities; (2) limited working day; (3) paid rest and vacations, and

227. One special case is the Law 8901 of 2000, sanctioned in the Province of Córdoba, which established as a general rule the principle of 'equivalent participation of genders' for the choice of candidates not only to elective public posts but also broadening its scope of application to every list corresponding to collegiate, executive, deliberative, control, selection, professional or disciplinary bodies. Now, there are more precedents of this nature in other Provinces and for the election of National Deputies of the Nation.

228. The recognition of the rights of women evolved steadily over time, beginning with the sanction of Law 11.357 on the civil rights of women (1926), as they were considered 'incapable' in the original Civil Code; then it moved into other fields, with the incorporation of international instruments reinforcing that legislation, such as the Convention on the Political Rights of Women (Law 15.786, 1960), and later the Convention on the Elimination of All Forms of Discrimination against Women (Law 23.179, of 3 Jun. 1985). The latter (Arts 2, 3, 4 and 7) imposes on the states the obligation to establish 'appropriate measures', including legislation, to make the provisions and rights embedded in it effectively feasible. These temporary measures should cease when the equal treatment and opportunities proposed are achieved. Finally, Law 23.592 punishes discriminatory acts or omissions determined by motives of gender, among various other assumptions.

ordinary or special leave; (4) fair payment; (5) adjustable minimum living wage; (6) equal pay for equal work; (7) protection against arbitrary dismissal; (8) family benefits; (9) economic improvement; (10) participation in licit activities that help to defend their professional interests; and (11) free, democratically based union organizations.

In addition to providing for these rights in Article 14*bis*, the Constitution also has other complementary norms on the matter in Article 75, Clauses 19 and 23. It recognizes the rights of women, the protection of childhood and pregnant women, and the rights of the disabled and of the elderly. And the Congress is empowered:

> To provide everything relevant to human development, economic progress with social justice, the growth of the national economy, the creation of jobs, the professional training of workers, the defense of the currency value, the scientific and technological research and development, their overall diffusion and beneficial use.

§4. Third-Generation Rights

127. The 1994 Constitutional Reform included the so-called third-generation rights in the chapter called 'New Rights and Guarantees'.

Thus, Article 41 says:

> All inhabitants are entitled to the right to a healthy and balanced environment fit for human development in order that productive activities shall meet present needs without endangering those of future generations; and shall have the duty to preserve it. As a first priority, environmental damage shall bring about the obligation to repair it according to law. The authorities shall provide for the protection of this right, the rational use of natural resources, the preservation of the natural and cultural heritage and of the biological diversity, and shall also provide for environmental information and education.

And Article 42 declares: 'As regards consumption, consumers and users of goods and services have the right to the protection of their health, safety and economic interests; to adequate and truthful information; to freedom of choice and equitable and reliable treatment.'

§5. Legal Position of Foreigners and Constitutional Protection of Minorities

128. Attracting foreign immigrants was one of the major thrusts of the constituents of 1853 (Articles 25 and 67, Clause 16, today 75, Clause 18) with the idea of populating the vast extensions of the Argentine territory.

This is why the civil rights of foreigners were recognized at the constitutional level (Article 20):

> Foreigners enjoy within the territory of the Nation all the civil rights of citizens; they may exercise their industry, trade and profession; own real property, buy and sell it; navigate the rivers and coasts; practice freely their religion; make wills and marry under the laws. They are not obliged to accept citizenship nor to pay extraordinary compulsory taxes.

Immigration policy was also established in Article 25:

> The Federal Government shall foster European immigration; and may not restrict, limit or burden with any tax whatsoever, the entry into the Argentine territory of foreigners who arrive for the purpose of tilling the soil, improving industries, and introducing and teaching arts and sciences.

Foreigners may obtain Argentine nationality. The Congress is empowered 'to enact general laws of naturalization and nationality for the whole nation, based on the principle of nationality by birth or by option for the benefit of Argentina' (Article 75, Clause 12). According to Article 8: 'The citizens of each province shall be entitled to all rights, privileges, and immunities inherent in the condition of citizen[s] in the other provinces … .'

129. Article 67, Clause 15 of the Constitution of 1853/1860 mandated Congress to: 'maintain peaceful treatment of the Indians and promote their conversion to Catholicism'. Thus, they aimed at the assimilation of the aboriginal peoples.

The Constitutional Reform of 1994, from a multicultural perspective in line with modern trends in human rights, stipulated in the current Article 75, Clause 17:

> To recognize the ethnic and cultural pre-existence of indigenous peoples of Argentina. To guarantee respect for the identity and the right to bilingual and intercultural education; to recognize the legal capacity of their communities, and the community possession and ownership of the lands they traditionally occupy; and to regulate the granting of other lands adequate and sufficient for human development; none of them shall be sold, transmitted or subject to liens or attachments. To guarantee their participation in issues related to their natural resources and in other interests affecting them. The provinces may jointly exercise these powers.

Progressively the courts, especially the provincial ones, apply these norms in their rulings, ensuring their enforcement given the lack of suitable regulation.[229]

229. *See*, for instance: 'Sede, Alfredo c/Vila Herminia', Juzg. 1ra. C., Com. y Min. Nª. 5, Bariloche (Río Negro), 12/8/2004; 'Comunidad Mapuche Huayquillan c/Brescia C.', Juzg. 1ºC., Com., Lab. Min., V Circ., Neuquén, 18/8/2004, and more recently, 2 Sentences of the Supreme Court of Justice of the Nation in 'Confederación Indígena del Neuquén c. Provincia del Neuquén s/Acción de inconstitucionalidad', 12/10/2013, Fallos 336:2271 and 'Martínez Pérez José Luis c. Palma Américo y otros s/medida cautelar s/casación', 11/10/2015.

Chapter 2. Guarantees

§1. Guarantees of Due Process

130. Throughout this work we have spoken about the system of rights and their protection in the legal order, within the federal organization of the Argentine State.

Albeit briefly, we have pointed out the double source of the rights, as well as the characteristics of the Argentine judicial branch, to which is added the possibility of the protection of rights through the regional and universal systems, provided for in the international treaties of human rights, some of which have constitutional rank and are part of our so-called block of federal constitutionality.

We have likewise referred briefly to the institutional processes that can be used before the federal and provincial courts and those of the Autonomous City of Buenos Aires for exercising constitutional judicial review, which is the most important function of any judge in the country. Needless to say, this diffuse control aims substantially to safeguard the supremacy of the constitutions, the most important aim of which, in turn, is to ensure the dignity of the human person, in accordance with the liberal, humanist and democratic philosophy emerging from their standards, principles and values.

Joaquín V. González wrote eloquently about this in his celebrated *Manual of Constitutional Law*:

> The declarations, rights and guarantees are not, as might be believed, simple theoretical formulas: each of the sections and clauses they contain have obligatory force for individuals, for the authorities and for all the Nation. The judges must apply them in the fullness of their sense, without altering or weakening the express significance of their text with vague interpretations or ambiguities, because they are the personal defence, the unchangeable patrimony that makes each person, citizen or otherwise, a free and independent being within the Argentine Nation.

For this reason, respect for the independence of the judicial branches is fundamental for the full currency of the Argentine rule of law and of human rights, and this is a cardinal principle of the republican, democratic system, along with the firm conviction of the judges about their exalted mission.

131. The Constitution expressly regulates guarantees about due process, defence in trial, proof, natural judge, protection of personal freedom and the inviolability of the home. Regarding these guarantees, Article 18 says:

> No inhabitant of the Nation may be punished without previous trial based on a law enacted before the act that gives rise to the process, nor tried by special committees, nor removed from the judges appointed by law before the act for which he is tried. Nobody may be compelled to testify against himself, nor be arrested except by virtue of a written warrant issued by a competent authority. The defense by trial of persons and rights may not be violated. The domicile

> may not be violated, as well as the written correspondence and private papers; and a law shall determine in which cases and for what reasons their search and occupation shall be allowed.

Likewise, Article 8 of the American Convention on Human Rights (Pact of San José de Costa Rica), applied domestically by Article 75, Clause 22 of the Constitution, regulates even more broadly the guarantees of due process. Article 25 of the pact includes the so-called judicial protection or effective due process, that is, guaranteed access to a simple, rapid and effective legal resource.

§2. Other Guarantees: Injunctions, Habeas Corpus and Habeas Data

132. We must stress the importance of the injunction within the guarantees to provide for and to ensure the full currency of fundamental rights. We recognize the primacy of Mexican constitutionalism in creating this notable institution in the nineteenth century, which then spread within Latin America and into the world.

In Argentine law, just as habeas corpus is the guarantee with the greatest historical lineage, aimed at preserving physical or mobile freedom, the injunction is the most important generic guarantee in relation to the other fundamental rights.

At the federal level, three stages can be identified: (a) its creation in a 'pretorian' manner, by the Supreme Court of the nation, in the decisions in *Siri Angel* of 1957 and *Kot SRL* of 1958, which admitted the injunction hearing against acts that harm fundamental rights arising from the state or from private persons, respectively; (b) the legislation of the institute through Law 16.986 of 1966, which restricted its scope; and (c) the constitutionalization of the injunction in Article 43, incorporated in the 1994 Constitutional Reform.[230]

This norm of the federal Supreme Law declares:

> Any person shall file a prompt and summary proceeding regarding constitutional guarantees, provided there is no other legal remedy, against any act or omission of the public authorities or individuals, which currently or imminently may damage, limit, modify or threaten rights and guarantees recognized by this Constitution, treaties or laws, with open arbitrariness or illegality. In such case, the judge may declare that the act or omission is based on an unconstitutional rule.

And the Article adds:

> This summary proceeding against any form of discrimination and about rights protecting the environment, competition, users and consumers, as well as about rights of general public interest, shall be filed by the damaged party, the

---

230. In the list of subjects in which the constitutionalism of the Provinces has been more advanced than the federal must also be included the recognition of this fundamental guarantee. *See* Sagüés (2006:41).

ombudsman and the associations which foster such ends, registered according to a law, determining the requirements and organization forms.

The National Constitution has thus admitted the classic injunction against the acts both of the state and of private persons and has expressly recognized the possibility that judges can declare norms unconstitutional that violate fundamental rights, both currently and imminently. Likewise, the second paragraph has recognized the so-called collective injunction, which has also meant a significant broadening of active legitimation for the defence of the rights indicated and those of 'collective incidence'.

Sagüés (2006:44–46) notes that there is a range of injunction pleas at the federal level: against acts or omissions of the public authority from Law 16.986; against acts or omissions of private persons, provided for in Articles 321 and 498 of the Civil and Commercial Code of Procedure of the Nation; the injunction for delays of the administration from Laws 19.549 and 21.686; the injunction plea for delays of the Federal Tax Administration and National Customs Administration from Laws 11.683 and 22.415 and amendments; the electoral injunctions of the National Electoral Code; the unions injunction from the Law of professional associations 23.551; and the environmental injunction from Law 25.675. He also mentions the 'inter-American' injunction, provided for in Article 25 of the American Convention on Human Rights or the Pact of San José de Costa Rica, which has constitutional rank in Argentina, as we noted previously.

We must not omit the extraordinary importance that the injunction achieved from the last emergency that took place at the end of 2001, when the establishment of the economic and financial so-called *corralito* led to the presentation of more than 400,000 legal actions of this kind, to deal with the confiscation produced by the Federal Government and the banks of some 70,000 million dollars in fixed term deposits (*see* Hernández, 2003a).

The injunction in Argentina presents two distinctive characteristics: (a) it does not operate against acts of the Judicial branch, and (b) the review by federal justice concerning an injunction presented to local justice can only be made by means of the extraordinary federal review to the National Supreme Court, which has established as one of its requirements that the 'definitive judgment' be that of the Higher Court or Supreme Court of the respective Province or of the Autonomous City of Buenos Aires.

133. Other specific guarantees included in Article 43 of the Constitution are the habeas corpus, habeas data and the secret nature of the sources of journalistic information that 'shall not be impaired'.[231]

Habeas data are really a special injunction (Gelli, 2001:338), which aim to safeguard rights such as that to privacy, image, good name and commercial reputation, personal and family identity, among others (Gelli, 2001:352–353). Article 43 thus declares:

---

231. Other specific guarantees are included in Arts 18 and 19, which protect personal freedom, privacy and intimacy, and Art. 17, which defines property as 'inviolable'.

> Any person shall file this action to obtain information on the data about himself and their purpose, registered in public records or data bases, or in private ones intended to supply information; and in case of false data or discrimination, this action may be filed to request the suppression, rectification, confidentiality or updating of said data.

Law 25.326 regulated the constitutional text, and case law has worked to detail the scope of the measure.

134. The aim of habeas corpus is to protect a person when the right affected is of personal freedom or freedom of movement. Its origins lie in the English Magna Carta of 1215.

In Argentina, the 'classic' habeas corpus arose from Article 18 of the historical Constitution, which states, 'Nobody may be … arrested except by virtue of a written warrant issued by a competent authority.' Law 23.098 (1984) regulates this guarantee, which after the 1994 Constitutional Reform was detailed in the text of Article 43, last paragraph, of the Constitution: 'When the right damaged, limited, modified, or threatened affects physical liberty … the action of habeas corpus shall be filed by the party concerned or by any other person on his behalf, and the judge shall immediately make a decision even under state of siege.'

Article 43 also regulates the so-called corrective habeas corpus, which occurs 'in case of an illegitimate worsening of procedures or conditions of detention'. Already since 1853, Article 18 of the Constitution provided:

> The prisons of the Nation shall be healthy and clean, for the security and not for the punishment of the prisoners confined therein; and any measure taken with the pretext of precaution which may lead to mortify them beyond the demands of security, shall render liable the judge who authorizes it.[232]

Finally, Article 43 also refers to habeas corpus 'in case of … forced missing of persons'. The tragic history of Argentina in the 1976–1983 period gave rise to this guarantee, which also includes the obligation of the state to account to the families about their missing persons (Gelli, 2001:371).

232. The Supreme Court in the *Verbitksy* case (2005) admitted a corrective habeas corpus filed by a civil association concerning prisons in the province of Buenos Aires.

Part V. Specific Problems

Chapter 1. Analysis of the Emergency Institutions in Our History[233]

§1. Institutions Regulated by the Constitution[234]

I. Federal Intervention

135. Article 6 of the Constitution declares:

> The Federal Government may intervene in the territory of the provinces in order to guarantee the republican form of government or to repel foreign invasions; and at the request of their constituted authorities, it may intervene to support or reestablish them, should they have been deposed by sedition or invasion from another province.

This Article is correlated with Article 5, which sets the basis for the exercise of constituent authority by the Provinces: 'under the republican, representative system, in accordance with the principles, declarations, and guarantees of the National Constitution, ensuring its administration of justice, municipal regime, and elementary education'.

The federal intervention was provided for extraordinary situations, of true institutional emergency, when the basic principles of this form of state are affected, which involves the coexistence of various orders of government. This extreme remedy, clearly protective of the federation as a union pact, uniquely empowers the Federal Government to suspend or limit the provincial autonomy guaranteed by the Constitution. Autonomy is the legal status par excellence of local States in a federal regime. So any disruption of it must be exceptional, temporary and restricted in scope. Unlike other federations, in Argentina there have been more than 150 federal interventions, which two-thirds of the time were arranged by a simple Decree of the President of the Republic, without the intervention of Congress. The institute aided the centralization of the country. For this reason, in the 1994 Constitutional Reform

233. For a more complete study of this topic, *see* our book *Las emergencias y el orden constitucional*, 2ª. Ed., Instituto de Investigaciones Jurídicas de la Universidad Autónoma de Mexico and Rubinzal-Culzoni Editions, Mexico (2003). Also *see Constitutionalism in times of emergency*, published by the Argentine Association for Constitutional Law and the International Association for Constitutional Law, Workshop in Córdoba, Argentina.

234. The decrees of necessity and urgency and delegated legislation were analysed in Part I, Ch. 4 of this work.

the competence of the Congress on the subject was established in Article 75, Clause 31. The Executive branch, Article 99, Clause 20, can impose it when the latter is in recess but at the same time must convene extraordinary sessions to approve or revoke it.[235]

The Constitution states that the Federal Government 'intervenes in the territory of the Provinces', which originated a practice in accordance with intervention consisting of sending representatives to solve the problem presented, exercising mediation, but in no way replacing the local authorities, who were elected through provincial autonomy. This practice was adjusted after a few decades to include completely different criterion that subjugated local autonomy, as it became common to remove the authorities elected by the people.

We believe it is necessary to regulate Article 6 of the Constitution in order to prevent in the future the serious damage caused to the Supreme Law by the misuse of this institution of emergency.[236]

II. State of Siege

136. Article 23 of the Constitution states:

> In the event of domestic disorder or foreign attack endangering the full enforcement of this Constitution and of the authorities hereby established, the province or territory which is in a turmoil shall be declared in state of siege and the constitutional guarantees shall be suspended therein. But during such a suspension the President of the Republic shall not pronounce judgment or apply penalties on his own. In such case, his power shall be limited, with respect to persons, to their arrest or transfer from one place of the Nation to another, should they not prefer to leave the Argentine territory.

The Constitution prescribed this for two very serious emergencies: war and domestic chaos, when referring to the two causes of 'domestic disorder' or 'foreign attack', which must also meet two requirements: (1) it must endanger together both the Constitution and the authorities created by it and (2) it must cause public disturbance.

Ziulu (2000:181) notes that in fifty-two cases declared between 1853 and 2000, 61% of them were made by Executive Decree. This meant the exercise of exorbitant authority by the Executive branch, with the evident decline in congressional function, to which was added a significant decay in individual rights and guarantees.

The institutional hardships experienced led to a state of emergency every two years and nine months, with a record length of eight years, eleven months and

235. *See* Hernández (1997a and 2003a).

236. On 3 Jun. 1992 as National Deputy representing the Province of Córdoba, I presented a bill titled 'Regimen para la intervención federal de las Provincias'. *See* Hernández (1995b).

twenty-two days for that declared by Decree 1368 on 6 November 1974 by President Martinez de Peron, which then continued during the subsequent de facto period until 28 October 1983.[237]

This use and abuse of this extraordinary institution produced extremely serious injury to the republican system, to the rule of law and to democracy in Argentina, as the authoritarian exercise of power led to the severe and profound violation of personal rights.

Since the *Alem* case, decided by the Supreme Court in 1893, it has been argued that the state of siege does not involve suspending the validity of the Constitution. On the contrary, it is declared to preserve it and secure it.

Since the restoration of democratic institutions in 1983, there have been four events that indicate a substantial advance in the constraints that this institute should have in its constitutional interpretation and application:

(a) the promulgation of Law 23.098 of habeas corpus in 1984, which, in addition to impeding the exercise of this guarantee during a state of siege, allows Judges through Article 4, Clause 1 to control even the legitimacy of its declaration;
(b) the consolidation of the case law that extends constitutional judicial review over the measure and encompasses not only the implementation of concrete actions in relation to individuals but also as regards the declaration of the act in its extrinsic forms of the Law or Decree in question and its requirements such as the express period and determination of the place;[238]
(c) the setting of new limits in the matter, through the constitutionalization of international treaties on human rights (Article 75, Clause 22.); and
(d) the effective reduction of the states of siege declared in these years.

III. Necessity and Urgency Decrees

137. This topic was analysed in Part I, Chapter 3, §2.

IV. Legislative Delegation

138. This topic was analysed in Part I, Chapter 3, §2.

§2. Institutions Forbidden by the Constitution: Article 29

139. The Constitution set in this norm:

> Congress may not vest on the National Executive Power – nor may the provincial legislatures vest on the provincial governors – extraordinary powers or the total public authority; it may not grant acts of submission or supremacy

237. *See* Ziulu (2000:208).
238. C.S., fallos en *Granada* and *Rodríguez Jorge Horacio*, of 1985.

> whereby the life, honour, or wealth of the Argentine people will be at the mercy of governments or any person whatsoever. Acts of this nature shall be utterly void, and shall render those who formulate them, consent to them or sign them, liable to be condemned as infamous traitors to their fatherland.

These institutions can never be used at all, and clearly not in emergencies. The Article is a protest rising from the depths of history, as Law Professor Agustín de Vedia said, and moreover, was written in letters of blood, as Law Professor José Manuel Estrada argued, in reference to the dictatorship of Juan Manuel de Rosas. The same happened during de facto governments.

The highlight of the norm is its profound republican sense of democracy, which rejects all forms of authoritarianism and sets limits to public action in defence of human rights.

§3. Institutions Not Regulated by the Constitution[239]

I. De Facto Government

140. The political and institutional emergencies have been so serious in Argentina that on several occasions they have led to the breakdown of the Constitution, through coups d'état that installed de facto governments, producing great harm to the rule of law.

Argentine institutional history unfortunately shows successive interruptions of constitutional order, beginning in 1862 with the victory of General Mitre in the battle of Pavón and increasing in the twentieth century with the overthrow of President Yrigoyen in 1930 by the armed forces, who returned to power in 1943, 1955, 1966 and 1976. To this must be added the 1962 coup that led to the replacement of President Frondizi by the Senate President Guido, who was not a de jure ruler.

The painful periods should also be remembered in which proscriptions were imposed that prevented the unrestricted validity of the principle of popular sovereignty, the only source of democratic legitimacy of governments under the basic law.

These governments were unconstitutionally confirmed by the case law of the Supreme Court, which also gradually expanded its recognition to the de facto legislation.[240]

The insertion of current Article 36 in the Constitutional Reform of 1994 was aimed to ensure the validity of the Constitution and prevent such severe harm to the rule of law. The rule states:

> This Constitution shall rule even when its observance is interrupted by acts of force against the institutional order and the democratic system. These acts shall

239. These institutions not covered in the Constitution are unconstitutional because they are outside the jurisdiction granted by the Supreme Law to the different branches of government. *See* Hernández (2003b:353–354).

240. *See* Hernández (2003a:49).

> be irreparably null. Their authors shall be punished with the penalty foreseen in Article 29, disqualified in perpetuity from holding public offices and excluded from the benefits of pardon and commutation of sentences. Those who, as a consequence of these acts, were to assume the powers foreseen for the authorities of this Constitution or for those of the Provinces, shall be punished with the same penalties and shall be civil and criminally liable for their acts. The respective actions shall not be subject to prescription. All citizens shall have the right to oppose resistance to those committing the acts of force stated in this Article.

As Vice Chair of the Drafting Committee, we said in the plenary of the Constitutional Convention:

> Let me say what the nature of this norm is that we will incorporate into the Constitution. We believe that we are dealing with constitutional criminal norms … we are talking about a protected legal good which appears with great clarity: the constitutional order. We define in the norm the criminal behavior and the protected legal good, we refer to the penalties and also refer to the Congress the drafting and application of other penalties in this respect.

And after indicating the deterrent effect of the rule and the importance of recognizing resistance to oppression as a listed right as well as reference to public ethics as a presupposition of democracy, we spoke about the constitutional order:

> we consider the constitutional order to be is the nation itself. This was the clear definition of the leaders of our country, Juan Maria Gutierrez, when he said that the Constitution was the Argentine Nation made law. Since the first moments of national identity in the formidable debate on May 22 at the Open Assembly of Buenos Aires, the ideas of liberty, equality, the Republic and federalism were integrated into the depths of Argentine nationality … . It is therefore appropriate to say that the idea of constitutional order and the defense of democracy, which is an essential value of our Constitution, mean unquestionably the defense of the best ideas that Argentine nationality has had … . In this sense, this norm is also a declaration at the highest level; it is based on the painful history we have lived and in the deep conviction that we have about the effectiveness of democracy for the times to come. It expresses the consensus of this great Constitutional Convention and we believe that it is highly valuable to incorporate it into the constitutional text.[241]

241. *Ibid.*, (1995:57–59).

II. Martial Law, State of Alert and Alarm, and State of Assembly[242]

141. Martial law applies the code of military justice for common crimes to civilians, excluding the laws and the ordinary courts. It is not an institution of free peoples (Bidart Campos, 1972:170). It is therefore unconstitutional, as is argued by the majority doctrine.

Until 1930, it was used on two occasions.[243] From the coup d'état of that year, it was used more often, for example, during the de facto governments of 1943, 1966 and 1969. Although in 1960 President Frondizi issued the plan 'Conintes', by which civilians accused of certain crimes were tried under military law.

The state of alert and alarm implies an institutional situation for preventing possible crises. It involves granting anticipated and limited powers to the state authorities to try to prevent the state of siege (Ziulu, 2000:173–174). It existed during the brief period of validity of the Constitutional Reform of 1949.

The state of assembly occurs 'in cases of grave danger to the public and especially of foreign danger [given] the rapid formation or concentration of an army and organizing the defense of the territory and its inhabitants' (Rébora, 2001:27). In Argentina, this has not occurred since the nineteenth century.

III. Police Power of Emergency

142. The police power is the power of the state at its various levels to limit the exercise of individual rights to ensure certain purposes, which vary from a narrow concept that includes security, health or morals to a broader concept that also adds the general welfare.

The exercise of this power, inasmuch as it concerns the regulation of personal rights, corresponds to the legislative branch, on the basis of the principles of legality and reasonableness of Articles 14, 19 and 28 of the Supreme Law.

The police power, which was supported by Argentine jurisprudence and doctrine for a long time, was newly incorporated in the Constitution explicitly in Article 75, Clause 30, in the 1994 Constitutional Reform, with a clear federal sense.

The strict criterion on police power, which, in addition to the previously noted purposes for the exercise of that power, paid special attention to preserving individual freedoms and rights, began to change based on the case law of the Court, particularly in *Ercolano v. Lanteri de Renshaw*, 1922, when it accepted the broad criteria, which included general welfare as a purpose, in line with the modifications made with the greater intervention of the state in the economy.

Thus, since that period, more than eighty years ago, an exercise of police power began, which was to increasingly restrict individual rights. In this context, as from 1934, the policing power of 'emergency' was configured as a new institute, in response to the successive economic emergencies occurring. This institute did not

242. *Ibid.*, (2003a:51–55).

243. In Salta in 1868 and in San Juan in 1869. The latter had more serious consequences because it was applied to execute Zacarías Segura, which had repercussions in the Federal Senate, where General Mitre made a famous speech. *See* Ziulu (2000:171).

have any constitutional validation,[244] but wás ratified by the case law of our highest court in successive rulings as mentioned following,[245] which endorsed the actions of each political power shift.

In *Ercolano*, the Court recognized the constitutionality of Law 11.157 of 1921 that had frozen the prices of rents.

In *Avico v. De la Pesa* decided in 1934, which officially recognizes the new institute, the Court declared the constitutionality of Law 11.741, which had extended for three years the mortgage obligations and reduced their interest to 6%. Lazzarini does well to point out (1991:1468) that in this case, Attorney General Dr Horacio Rodriguez Larreta, following the standard of the US Court, listed the conditions for intervention in an emergency: (1) that an emergency situation imposes on the state a duty to protect the vital interests of the community; (2) that the law has the legitimate purpose of protecting the general interests of society and not specific individuals; (3) that the moratorium is reasonable, providing a relief justified by the circumstances; and (4) that its duration is temporary and limited to the time necessary to eliminate the causes that made the moratorium possible.

In *Inchauspe Hnos v. Junta Nacional de Carnes*, ruled in 1944, the Court upheld the constitutionality of a provision of Law 11.747 that provided for a compulsory contribution of 1.5% of the sale price of livestock, with producers being automatically converted to shareholders of the Argentine Meat Producers' Corporation, the goal of which was to compete with foreign cold storage firms in the monopoly of the meat business.

In *Vincent Martini e. hijos*, resolved in 1944, the High Court upheld the constitutionality of Law 12.591 of price caps, arguing that emergency situations authorize the exercise of policing power in the strongest terms.

In *Russo v. Delledonne*, decided in 1959, the Court declared the constitutionality of Article 1 of Law 14.442, which was extended by Laws 14.556 and 14.775, which paralyzed the trials and launches of evictions.

That same day the *Nadur* case was resolved and from both arises the legal doctrine that sets out the four requirements for an emergency that had been anticipated, as we saw, by the Attorney General Rodriguez Larreta.[246]

In *Cine Callao*, tried in 1960, the High Court granted the constitutionality of Law 14.226, which obliged the inclusion of live variety shows in cinemas on the occasion of showing films, to alleviate the unemployment of the respective artists.

In *D Aste v. Caja Nacional de Previsión, Provident Fund*, decided in 1967, the Court accepted the constitutionality of Law 16.931 that had declared that the funds of National Provident Funds were unattachable and had paralyzed for sixteen months the process of trials for charging of pension adjustments.

Thus, we come to the famous *Peralta* case, decided by our High Court in 1990, which ratified the previous judicial doctrine in the matter of emergency and also endorsed for the first time the issue of decrees of necessity and urgency, through the

---

244. *See* Ekmekdjian (1883:617); Midón (2001:93).

245. *See* Maljar (2002), Lazzarini (1991) and Colautti (1991), whom we follow in the presentation of the cases.

246. Midón (2001:93). In turn, Colautti (1991:1360) indicates that these guidelines were established by the US Supreme Court case *Home Building & Loan v. Blaisdell* (1934) and it has subsequently maintained them.

Decree 36/90 which had decided on the Plan Bonex, which meant the seizure of bank deposits and their compulsory exchange for bonds at a period of ten years.[247]

In addition to this, and as Midón relates (2001:56) in a critical position that we share, the High Court invoked an 'authentic interpretation' as opposed to a 'static' interpretation 'that meant the paralyzing of government action and of the progress of the republic' and on this basis accepted the validity of the decree of necessity and urgency, basing its determination on two central reasons: (1) because the National Congress, in the exercise of its own constitutional powers, does not take different decisions on the points of economic policy involved and (2) because there has been a situation of serious social risk, against which there was a need for acute measures of the kind implemented in the decree, the efficacy of which does not seem conceivable by means other than those decided. As if this were not enough, the Court even held that the principle of separation of powers is a 'historical category'.

As will be appreciated, this decision is for us a remarkable example of the complacent attitude that the High Court developed over more than eighty years in this field of economic emergency, despite the excesses committed by the executive and legislative branches (the latter by action or omission) against the republican system and individual rights.

For this reason, the decision of Attorney General of the Court Dr Sebastian Soler in the *Cine Callao* case in 1960 stands out; he indicated that with these attitudes nothing would remain that was important for the rule of law, which led to the mood of the people feeling that a strict system of law was not compatible with progress.[248]

143. This brings us to the *latest economic emergency*, originating in late 2001 and continuing for 16 years, which gave rise to the popularly named financial and banking *corralito*[249] and also produced the most serious constitutional violations through the use of this type of institutions.

But unlike what happened on previous occasions, the mission of the judiciary, consisting essentially in exercising constitutional judicial review, was assumed by the Supreme Court in the case of *Smith*, decided on 1 February 2002, which

247. For the analysis of this case, *see* Lazzarini (1991), Colautti (1991), Pérez Hualde (1995, 2002a and 2002b) and Midón (2001:54).

248. Supreme Court of Justice, Judgments, 247:121.

249. The *corralito* had two versions: the first, ordered by the decree of necessity and urgency 1570 of 2001, established limits for the withdrawal of bank deposits, and the second, ordered by the decree of necessity and urgency 214 of 2002, saw the confiscation of these deposits, in addition to the change of currency. These deposits reached 65,000 million Dollars and Pesos, affecting about 5 million savers, 90% of whom had deposits that did not exceed USD 50,000, which indicates that they belong to the middle and lower economic classes of society.

The *corralito* included these aspects: (a) confiscation of deposits of millions of savers; (b) the investigation of wrongful acts committed in this process; and (c) the liquidation of the liabilities of the economically most powerful sectors of the country with the pesification that occurred by the same Decree 214. The *corralito* signified not only the violation of property rights but also of a wide range of individual rights and guarantees, as well as damage to the republican system and rule of law. There was an extraordinary popular reaction against these measures, which resulted in the fall of President De la Rua and a sharp political crisis, in addition to the presentation of more than 400,000 injunctions before Federal Judiciary. For a full analysis, *see* Hernández (2003a: 71).

declared unconstitutional the first version of the *corralito* and in favour of the federal Judges who had granted injunctions for savers in cases brought by those who suffered the confiscation of their deposits.[250] Subsequently, the Supreme Court ruled unconstitutional the second version of the *corralito*, established by the Decree of necessity and urgency 214, in the case of *Provincia de San Luis*, sentenced on 5 March 2003.[251]

That independent action of the Judiciary, which set limits to the provisions of the Executive and Legislative branches, along with the massive and unprecedented use of the injunction enshrined in Article 43 of the Constitution, constituted, from our perspective, the most striking aspect of the difficult period of the rule of law in the distressing reality of Argentina. However, the new membership of the Supreme Court, after the nominations of President Kirchner, based on the *Bustos* and *Cabrera* cases of 2004 and *Massa* in 2006, returned to the previous case law convalidating the economic emergency.[252]

We also reiterate that, unfortunately, the Congress has every year since 2003 extended the Emergency Economic Law 25.561, which produced the most serious legislative delegation that we have suffered.

§4. The Decline of Our Rule of Law and the Urgent Need to Subordinate Emergencies to the Constitutional Order

144. The previous analysis of the whole of Argentine institutional history shows conclusively that:

(a) In response to the various emergencies suffered, different institutions of emergency were used, provided for, not provided for or prohibited by the Constitution.
(b) The exercise of these institutions produced severe injury to our rule of law, constitutional order, the republican system and to individual rights.
(c) In all the cases observed when these institutions were used, the executive branch acted exaggeratedly, intensifying the hyperpresidentialism we have suffered.
(d) The Legislative branch has also been responsible for these deviations institutional acting in this way, either actively or passively or by omission, since in some cases it accompanied by policies of the Executive, through the adoption of the respective laws or making delegations in that and other cases, by not realizing any political control of the measures, thus abdicating its essential functions.
(e) As regards the Judicial branch, except for the exceptional cases mentioned, no correct and strong exercise was seen of its powers of judicial review, which

250. In this regard, note the clear rationale of the Court in the *Smith* case found in Considerations 9 and 10 of the ruling. There the idea reflects constitutional judicial review over the emergency, based on the limits of reasonability of s. 28, to prevent injury to individual rights. In this sense, we cannot ignored the fact that the Court changed with this ruling the complacent case law of any emergency measure dictated by any political power, as noted throughout many decades.
251. *See* Hernández (2003a:119).
252. *Ibid.*, (2007b:70).

showed its lack of independence and of fulfilling its role as a power of the republican state.[253] Faced with this painful diagnosis of the decline of Argentine rule of law, we believe that it is urgent to subordinate the different types of emergencies and institutions to the Constitution, as corresponds to the constitutional and democratic rule of law.

In this regard, we especially remember the guidelines of limitation and control, noted years ago by Germán J. Bidart Campos, based on conciliation between the effectiveness of reasonably chosen means to overcome the emergency and to protect individual rights and freedoms:

(a) Prior to the enactment of an institution of emergency or the adoption of the respective measures, the competent authority should make a formal declaration on the state of emergency.
(b) It is advisable that this declaration, as well as the establishment of the institution of emergency, should be subject to constitutional judicial review.
(c) It is appropriate that the authority express the reasons underlying the declaratory act of such measures, so that the control can operate in an objective and reasonable manner.
(d) The extent of the institution of emergency measures in time and space should be set.
(e) The three branches of government should remain in full operation and keep the constitutional judicial review, as any violation of rights caused by the emergency has to be judiciable, in order to respect the effective judicial protection.

145. Ultimately, we believe that emergencies and their institutions must adapt to the principles and rules of our constitutional, liberal and republican order; therefore, even though the Executive may have greater capacity to tackle the exceptional situation, this does not mean that Congress should not participate in the deliberation and decision of the measures to be taken, and also to ensure in particular the possibility of judicial review to protect individual guarantees and safeguard the constitutional supremacy.[254]

We understand that this involves a delicate balance between democratic legitimacy and the effectiveness of the measures designed to avert the emergency, but that is the challenge that must be assumed in order not to continue applying the formulas of the past, which have produced an obvious decline in the constitutional supremacy. To the latter has been added a notable lack of effectiveness in resolving emergencies, which, in addition to affecting democratic legitimacy, has led to passing from one emergency to another in a state of permanent crisis.

We believe that we must subordinate the emergency and its institutions to the basic law and limit its scope. To achieve these purposes, profound cultural, political, social and educational changes are necessary, which are the subject of another

253. *See* Bidart Campos (1972:166–167).
254. We are convinced that the Judicial branch must play a highly significant role in the change that we need, establishing suitable criteria for monitoring presidential power.

analysis, but one that is essential to tackle in order to overcome the anomia that is 'essentially antidemocratic', as Nino explained.[255]

To complete this essay, we believe that this phrase of Hume was well remembered recently:[256] 'A principle separates civilization from barbarism: pacta sunt servanda.' Therefore, we should not forget that the most important of our pacts is the Constitution, the supremacy and normative force of which we must ensure.

255. According to Nino (1992b:272), 'Democracy requires the enforcement of the rules that have been passed by majority rule after a process of discussion.' Ultimately, anomie is the context of our social life and partly explains our underdevelopment, which is a deficiency in the realization of democracy. It implies the existence of pockets of authoritarianism and anarchy in a formally democratic context.

256. Hutchinson (2002:27).

Chapter 2. The Constitutional Culture in Argentina[257]

§1. The Concept of Constitutional Culture

146. We owe the most in-depth studies on the connections between culture and the Constitution to the German Professor Peter Häberle.[258] The author maintains that the 'Constitution is not limited to just being a set of legal texts or a mere collection of laws, but that it expresses a certain degree of cultural development, a means of an entire people's personal self-representation, a mirror of their cultural legacy and the bedrock of their hopes and desires.'[259] And he adds 'the juridical side of every constitutional State is only a fragment of the reality of every living Constitution which, throughout its entire text and context, is only one of that State's cultural expressions. That is why the actual texts of a Constitution must be literally "cultivated" (the noun culture comes from the Latin verb cultivare) in order to become an authentic Constitution'.[260]

So the eminent Professor defines constitutional culture as 'the sum of attitudes and ideas, subjective experiences, scales of values, subjective expectations and the corresponding objective actions both at the personal level of a citizen and his associations, as well as at the level of government organizations and any others related with the Constitution'.[261]

Logically, then, this survey is targeted at finding out citizens' attitudes, perceptions and values regarding basic law and legality in general, to determine what our constitutional culture is like.

§2. Violation of the Laws in Argentina

147. People have pointed to the anomy problem in Argentina from different perspectives,[262] but we shall concentrate especially on those who have done so from the legal viewpoint.

---

257. We follow our books 'Encuesta de Cultura Constitutional. Argentina una sociedad anómica', dirigido por Antonio María Hernández, Daniel Zovatto and Manuel Mora y Araujo, Instituto de Investigaciones Jurídicas de la UNAM e IDEA International, Méjico, 2005 (*see* Hernández (2005) y 'Segunda Encuesta de Cultura Constitucional. Argentina una sociedad anómica', Antonio María Hernández, Daniel Zovatto y EduardoFidanza Compiladores, Eudeba, Buenos Aires, 2016.
258. In particular in Häberle (2000). In the original edition, published in 1982 in Berlin, Germany, titled *Verfassungslehre als Kulturwissenschaft*, Duncker & Humblot, the distinguished Professor condenses his thinking into ten thesis.
259. Häberle (2000:34).
260. *Ibid.*, (2000:35).
261. *Ibid.*, (2000:36–37).
262. Noteworthy among our most representative literary works is *Martín Fierro*, by José Hernández, in which references are made to unjust laws – that benefit the rich and powerful – to the need to befriend judges, and to 'native cleverness', in an outstanding story about the life of a gaucho at odds with society and its laws in the nineteenth century. And in Argentine folk music, no one can ignore the trenchant lyrics of Enrique Santos Discépolo's tango 'Cambalache,' which constitutes a sociological description and appraisal of the breakdown of our laws and values in the twentieth century.

In his well-known book *La ciudad Indiana*, focused on research of Argentine history in the seventeenth and eighteenth centuries, Juan Agustín García, Law Professor of the University of Buenos Aires, indicated that one of the four sentiments of that era was 'contempt or disregard for the Law'.[263]

In reference to the law in colonial times, he said:

> theoretical law was admirable for its charitable benevolence; the royal letters patent recommended good treatment, education and conversion of the Indians. But, alas, all over Hispanic America consultation of written law is the least important and illustrative: the Law, good or bad, grows and develops from the ground up, amid conflict of passions and interests, and protecting the most powerful inhabitants. Generally despicable, biased and cruel, it is propelled by ignominious sentiments and fierce self-interests.[264]

Besides pointing out the arbitrariness of councils in their regulation of trade and monopolies, he mentioned paternalism as another characteristic, which forced the population to depend on a monarch viewed as an 'incarnation of Providence on earth'.[265]

García described the practice of the all-embracing power of the colonial authorities, with no rights for the gaucho, which kindled:

> deep within the Gaucho soul a feeling of contempt for the Law: in his imagination the Law is the symbol of arbitrariness, the use of capricious and discretionary brute force, incarnated in a bossy, somewhat cruel, greedy extortionate official, a 'petty mayor' ... always willing to bend justice in favor of the prestigious hacienda owner with connections in the capital ... . He knows he has no rights, that is, he has the clear impression that his welfare, his things, his family are minutiae that the official machine tramples over without the slightest concern.[266]

Later the author wrote of the struggle that began in the colonial era between the individual and the government: 'it reached a peak with the caudillos, troops of

---

263. *See* García (1909). José Manuel Estrada raised this sharp observation at the beginning of the book: 'If we could truly know the ins and outs of the colonial society, we would solve three quarters of the problems that weigh us down.' The first reference to contempt for the law being a national sentiment is included in the Preface of the book, 7.
264. García (1909:34–35), chapter on *Las campañas*.
265. García (1909:151), chapter on *La administración de la ciudad* [Administration of the City]. The author claims that town councils were a 'sad parody of the Castilian councils destroyed by Charles V after Villalar battle' (p. 157), and 'that councilors were appointed by their outgoing predecessors, with approval from the governor, who also sometimes appointed them' (p. 164). In addition, the author compares them with those of the United States, underscoring the contrast with a reality evidenced by constitutional letters and political practices that showed an eager defence of ideals, interests and government itself.
266. García (1909:262–263), in the chapter on *El proletariado en las campañas* [The Proletariat in the Campaigns].

mounted rebels and anarchy, a supreme victory for individualism'.[267] In conclusion, he indicated that the essential traits of our political law are 'the predominance of the classical State-providence concept, political centralization, inferior and subordinate role of assemblies; and in the population, accentuating and fortifying those traits, a disregard for the law converted into instinct, into a motive for free will'. He followed by saying: 'One can state, without fear of falling into a paradox, that the country has not come out of the old regimen.'

We end this brief recollection of his thoughts with a sentence we also believe to be decidedly and disturbingly contemporary: 'Now, as before, higher-learning studies have dropped off, especially law studies! Does that make it a bad thing, for heaven's sake, to broadcast the Law?'[268]

Undoubtedly the best study of anomy made in Argentina was written by Carlos Santiago Nino, Law Professor at the National University of Buenos Aires, in his book *Un país al margen de la ley* [A Lawbreaking Country].[269]

Using an interdisciplinary perspective, Nino demonstrated with irrefutable intellectual brilliance why Argentina had a lawless history and how that also produced its underdevelopment.[270] The book's main thesis purported to show how anomy in itself worked to produce deficiency.[271]

Quoting Jon Elster's idea that 'laws are the cement of society', he maintained that laws 'make the integrity and subsistence of societies possible', and therefore 'lawlessness and anomy in general affect social productivity, at least in a capitalist system', as Max Weber showed.[272]

---

267. García (1909:298–299), in the chapter on *La administración de la capital* [Administration of the Capital].
268. García (1909:365–366), *Conclusión* [Conclusion].
269. Nino (1992b).
270. Nino (1992b:24) said: 'This trend towards anomy, or more specifically towards lawlessness, largely involves factors marked as pivotal for explaining the involution of Argentina's development, not to mention their having a separate causative effect.' He maintained that anomy in Argentina was quite easy to perceive as it gradually arose from the massive violation of human rights in the 1970s through government terrorism and left-wing terrorism. But he also mentioned a less dramatic case: that of the society's external image projected during transit in streets and highways, in the cleanliness of public places or in urban aesthetics (*see* p. 25). Then, after referring to other aspects, such as corruption or the involution of economic growth, he mentioned political instability in these terms: 'Such political instability culminated in the coups d'état which obviously marked the height of Argentine lawbreaking. But there are other more indirect ways in which political instability was related with lawbreaking: the electoral frauds, like those practiced prior to the Sáenz Peña Law and during the infamous decade; also, the electoral proscriptions such as the one that occurred first with the radicalism of that same decade, and again with Peronism from 1958 to 1973. The abuse of federal interventions, the president's usurpation of Congress's faculties, the manipulation of justice, abusive martial law, seriously affected the partisan legitimacy of Argentina's political system and, consequently, also contributed to society's weak support for it – a prerequisite for its subversion by force.' (Nino, 1992b:28).
271. Nino (1992b).
272. Nino (1992b:31–32). He quoted Max Weber in his book *La ética protestante y el espíritu del capitalismo* [Protestant Ethics and the Spirit of Capitalism], where he says: 'modern, rational industrial capitalism needs both the technical means for job calculation, as well as foreseeable rights and an administration guided by formal regulations. Without this, adventurous, commercial, speculative capitalism, not to mention every kind of political capitalism, is indeed possible; but private commercial industry with fixed capital and safe calculation is impossible'.

Furthermore, he introduced a new assessment of anomy to explain the Argentine case; he named it 'dumb' because disregard for laws was affecting values such as security and the ability to make forecasts and was producing a deficient collective action.[273]

With stinging precision he then referred to anomy in the institutional and social life of Argentina, to laws that are like tools for cooperation. To escape from the anomy trap, he was proposing a process of public discussion and education of the masses to promote loyalty to the law.[274]

Finally, Nino described anomy as antidemocratic because it involves violation of laws that must be sanctioned by a majority ruling after a debating process. And in our case it meant a deficiency in the materialization of democracy by insinuating the existence of pockets of authoritarianism.[275]

In my book *Las emergencias y el orden constitucional* [Emergencies and Constitutional Order] I purport the thesis that throughout history emergency institutions have usually been used to violate the constitutional system, the republican order and the enforcement of human rights.[276] In the initial words of that book I say:

> Over the last few months, we Argentines have lived through a tremendous crisis that has shaken the structure of all aspects of national life. Faced with this situation, we have been thinking for quite some time that we need to look inside ourselves to see what we are like, both individually and as a society, so as to understand how one of the countries with the greatest prospects at the beginning of the 20th century could end up in the embarrassing situation we now find ourselves. And then, after formulating a diagnosis, we must try to plan a different future more in keeping with the projects and dreams we initially had as a country.
>
> We are convinced that such a formidable task will take humility, decisiveness and exemplary ethics to change individual and mass behavior and values. Consequently, education, science and technology must become key instruments for this process, in tune with the information age we live in.
>
> Taking into account our responsibility as constitutional law professors and lawyers committed to defending the individual rights of affected persons, we consider that the best action we can take in this painful situation is to contribute to the study and discussion of one of the problems that most hurts us: anomy.
>
> Not long ago, in a remarkable must-read book titled *Un país al margen de la ley* [A Lawbreaking Country], Carlos S. Nino clearly showed – using a mixture of law, philosophy and sociology – why Argentina is a country with a pronounced general proclivity for lawlessness and why it was one cause of our under-development.

---

273. Nino (1992b:40).
274. Nino (1992a), Chs 2, 3, 5 and 6, respectively. We particularly recommend reading them.
275. Nino (1992b:272), *Epílogo* [Epilogue].
276. Hernández (2003a).

Now, with the same intention he had, but from a more juridical-constitutional perspective, this essay of ours will focus on analyzing emergency processes and constitutional order, to try to demonstrate from this standpoint how and why our rule of law decayed during our institutional history, and how we can make changes now and in the future to permanently uphold the values of the constitutional and democratic rule of law.

We are convinced that, while this particular experience cannot be applied to other Latin American countries, it can, however, be said that emergency situations and constitutional order in general have been common to our constitutional realities, producing similar outcomes as far as the unrestricted enforcement of the rule of law is concerned.

§3. Perceptions about the Law and the Constitution[277]

I. Lack of Respect for the Law

A. Argentina, the Argentine People and the Law

148. In Argentina, perceptions of a lack of respect for the law run high. In the first survey in 2004, only 11% of the people polled estimated that the laws and the Constitution are respected, whereas 86% maintained that Argentines live most of the time on the wrong side of the law. Moreover, only 8% of citizens respected the laws and the Constitution, and 88% rated themselves as transgressors.

These basic conclusions are common to all sectors polled because no great difference is evident in the opinions of groups varying by age, residence, gender or education. What is evident, though, is the fact that awareness of this lack of respect for the law among young people is greater among those who are less educated. Curiously, although 86% of those with high school or higher levels of education think that Argentines are transgressors, and that percentage rises to 90% among those who have not completed secondary school.

B. Obeying the Law

149. Despite these figures, when asked to what extent the different social actors abide by the law, a majority of people (82%) claim that they do and instead accuse the rest of the people of failing to do so (only 32% credit them with obeying the law). This perception is even bleaker regarding the national government because only 22% see it as law abiding. Worse still is the opinion of provincial governments, claimed to respect the law by only 19% of interviewed.

277. According the First Survey on Constitutional Culture made in Argentina in 2004, directed by Antonio María Hernández, Daniel Zovatto and Manuel Mora y Araujo, and published in 2005 in the Book 'Encuesta de Cultura Constitucional. Argentina: una sociedad anómica', before cited.

Again there is a divide between the 18- and 29-year age group and the over-60s with regard to respect for the law; the former amounted to 77%, the latter 89%. A similar variation is seen in terms of gender: male 80%, female 85%.

As for the national or Federal Government and respect for the law, the perception is not uniform across the different groups. Only 17% of young people between 18 and 29 believe the government respects the law, whereas 27% of people over 60 do so. An average of 22% is found in the intermediate groups of 30–44-year-olds and 23% in 45–59-year-olds. There is some uniformity in the perceptions of those who live in the metropolitan area (21%) and provincial cities (23%), who credit the government with respect for the law.

This same conclusion of the groups is observed concerning provincial governments and respect for the law, with an average of 19%. While the percentage of young people estimating provincial compliance with the law reaches 15%, among older people that percentage is 22%. In the metropolitan area, this perception reaches 14%, and in the provincial cities 21%.

Interviewees' impressions about provincial governments and the law also vary depending on the cities in which the polls were conducted. While an average of 19% was seen in the cities of Buenos Aires, San Miguel de Tucumán and Mar del Plata, there are two capitals with a perception of higher respect for the law: Mendoza at 25% and Córdoba at 23%. In other cities, it is less: 18% in Rosario and only 12% in the metropolitan area.

C. Reasons Why the Law Is Obeyed

150. When they were asked why the law is obeyed, 44% of the people polled replied that they respect the law because it is a moral duty, 37% because it benefits everyone, 9% in order not to harm family and friends, 8% to avoid punishment and 1% in order not to be criticized by others.

In the first answer, there was no uniformity among the different groups: whereas 41% of young people say they respect the law as their moral duty, the over 60-year-olds reached 51%; in the metropolitan area the figure was 42%, in the interior, 47%; men registered 42% and women 47%. These figures show a greater proportion of respect for the law for moral reasons among older people, residents in the interior and women.

In the second answer, again there was no uniformity in the percentage of the different groups. The data show greater consciousness of the common good – obeying the law is presumed to benefit everyone – among the 45–59-year-old age group, residents in the metropolitan area and those who have completed high school studies or more. Whereas 34% of young people saw the common benefit, 42% of the 45–59-year-old group did so. Residents of the metropolitan area showed 40%, compared to 33% in the provincial cities. People with unfinished secondary or high school studies showed 35%, whereas those with high school studies and more showed 41%.

Of the third percentage of replies – obeying the law so as not to harm family and friends (overall 9%) – 7% came from the metropolitan area, compared to 11% from the provincial cities. And for the fourth percentage – obeying the law so as to avoid punishment (overall 8%) – the figure rises to 13% in the youth sector.

D. Exceptions in Law Enforcement

151. The sentence 'There are times when it is necessary to disobey the law' triggered 48% of responses in disagreement and 8% very much in disagreement, but it is important to note that there were 36% of affirmative answers and 5% very much in agreement. That means that 41% of the people polled admitted it was necessary to disobey the law at certain times.

Notable among the people who disagreed were 45–59-year-olds, residents in provincial cities and women.

The sentence 'Breaking the law isn't so bad; the bad part is getting caught' brought in 60% of answers of disagreement and 26% very much in disagreement, and showed the highest percentages in the same groups as for the previous question. What did stand out were the figures of 10% in agreement and 2% very much in agreement with this statement, coming mainly from the youngest sectors.

E. Universal Enforcement of the Law

152. This crucial topic of universal law enforcement was analysed by asking the following question: 'In your opinion, is it fair or unfair to enforce the law strictly if a person … ?' The different suppositions completing the question were as follows: sells drugs, pollutes the environment, batters a family member, drives through a red light, illegally hooks up to a power line to steal electricity, consumes drugs and fails to pay taxes.

The general observation was that there were high percentages in favour of strict law enforcement in the cases of drug sales (95%), pollution of the environment (91%), battering a family member (91%) and driving through a red light (82%), whereas for the other suppositions the percentages dropped: stealing electricity (67%), consuming drugs (64%) and failing to pay taxes (63%). Opinions were similar throughout the different groups interviewed.

Nevertheless the percentage is greater among women when it comes to enforcing the law strictly in the case of battering a family member; whereas in the case of drug consumption, the percentage is lower among young people, those residing in the metropolitan area and those who are more highly educated.

So there is evidence of an attitude that coincides with the lack of respect for the law previously observed in the first questions in the poll.

F. Lawbreaking

153. In this aspect, the results of the poll are of great concern because it is evident that the biggest lawbreakers, in total answers, are perceived to be, in descending order: first, politicians, with 74%; second, the police, with 56%; third, public officials, with 49%; fourth, the judges, with 41%; fifth, the general population, with 27%; sixth, lawyers, with 19%, and seventh, everyone, with 5%.

The perception that politicians and the police break the law increases among the youngest sector of the population, with men and people with higher education mentioning politicians in the greatest percentage. The metropolitan area and intermediate age groups contain a higher percentage of people who believe that public officials break the law more frequently.

Older people, residents in provincial cities and men show the highest percentage of people who think lawyers break the law.

G. Protection Against Abuses of Authority

154. On this important question, the perception of 90% of the people polled is that people are insufficiently protected against abuses of government authority. This extremely high percentage rises to 92% among young people, residents in provincial cities and people with more education.

II. Knowledge of the Constitution

A. Significance of the National Constitution

155. A majority of interviewees replied spontaneously to the question about this theme, and the accumulation of answers indicated preferentially these concepts: 'that which rules the country, society and living together' (20%); 'the absolute maximum instrument' (19%); 'something that must be obeyed' (16%); and 'a set of norms, regulations, laws' (14%). To a lesser degree, other answers were 'rights and obligations' (11%), 'a book that nobody wants to obey or law that nobody wants to obey' (5%), 'a government measure' (2%), 'do not know' (13%) and 'no answer' (3%).

The perception of the significance of the Constitution is thus only barely relative in the country because a considerable number of replies reveal no knowledge of it.

B. Importance of the National Constitution

156. A total of 89% considered it very important (52%) and important (37%), compared with 11% who attributed little (8%) or no importance (2%) to it, or who did not know (1%). Older people, residents in provincial cities and those with higher education are the sectors who assign the most importance to the Constitution.

C. Respecting the National Constitution

157. A large percentage of the population (85%) acknowledges no respect for the Constitution (19% no respect, 66% little respect). This is a general conviction among the different groups polled. Only 13% think the Constitution is obeyed to some extent (11%) or to a high degree (2%).

D. Constitutional Rights Most Violated

158. The interviewees' perceptions of the most violated rights, by total mentions and in descending order, are as follows: first, the right to work (65%); second, to learn (28%); third, to complain, go on strike or hold protests (20%); fourth, to move around and circulate freely (17%); fifth, to teach (14%); sixth, free press and freedom of expression (10%); seventh, to do business and own property (7% each); eighth, to practise any religion (2%); and ninth, to associate with whomever one wishes (1%).

The highest percentage of opinions about violations of the right to work is seen in the metropolitan area, but this concern is common to all groups.

The highest percentage of opinions about violations of the right to learn is seen in the metropolitan area, in women and in people with higher education.

The highest percentage of opinions about violations of the right to complain is seen among young people and residents in provincial cities.

The highest percentage of opinions about violations of the right to travel around freely is seen in the metropolitan area and in people over 60.

Finally, people with higher education are the most concerned about violations to property rights.

E. Knowledge of the National Constitution

159. Practically 77% of the people polled say they have no knowledge of the National Constitution, adding those who know little (62%) or nothing (15%) about it. However, 22% declare some knowledge of it, ranging between fair (19%) and very good (3%). A greater proportion of senior citizens (23%) and those with a better education (34%) claim to have a fair knowledge of the Constitution.

The highest indicators of a poor knowledge of the Constitution are seen in young people and those between 45 and 59 years of age, in residents of provincial cities and in people who have not completed secondary school studies.

The highest percentages of people claiming to know nothing of the Constitution are those who have less education. Here, it is evident that the degree of knowledge of the Constitution is closely linked to educational levels.

To the question asking in which year the National Constitution was enacted, only 28% of the answers were correct, with a large gap between the less-educated group (only 14% correct answers) and people with high school educations and higher-learning diplomas (51%).

The question asking the year of the last constitutional reform drew 30% of correct answers and, as in the previous case, a big difference between the group of non-completed secondary school studies (18%) and the better educated group (48%).

The question about changes incorporated into the last reform also produced a disappointing result in the overall answers: on sixty-nine occasions, the answer was 'do not know' and on four there was no answer. Among those who answered about some of the topics, sixteen mentioned presidential re-election; four, the duration of mandates; three, the labour reform; one, children's rights; one, international human rights treaties; one, the education law; one, one additional senator; one, the Electoral College reform for direct vote by the President and Vice President; and one, other reforms.

F. Publicizing the National Constitution

160. The question about who first talked to citizens about the National Constitution drew the answers 'in school' (85% of answers) and 'at home' (9%), which reaffirms the importance of civic education.

To the question about where you hear the Constitution discussed today, there were sixty-eight mentions of the media, followed by forty, in school; twenty, in the home; fourteen, in the workplace; three, in church; and twelve, nowhere.

The answers mentioning school are more numerous among young people, women and people with more education.

G. Reform of the Constitution

161. Fifty-six per cent of the people polled replied that the Constitution should be reformed, whereas 30% said it should be left as is, and 13% professed not to know. The groups more inclined towards reform are young people between 18 and 29, residents in the interior, women and people who have completed secondary school education.

Among the group who claimed to know nothing about the Constitution, answers to the question about reform reached 53% in agreement. To the question about who should participate in the reform of the Constitution, 88% said the citizens, 66% the indigenous population, 65% non-government organizations, 63% Congress, 62% the government, 61% the President, 40% the political parties and 39% church representatives. Surprisingly, 55% of the people polled opposed the idea of political parties participating in the reform, followed by 54% opposing participation by representatives of the different churches.

To the question about whether people unfamiliar with laws should participate in the reform, 50% approve, compared to 41% who do not and 7% who replied 'to some extent'. The first opinion garners its biggest support from people with a higher education levels, whereas the opposite opinion has the support of people with lesser education.

Finally, noticeable here too is the high degree of unfamiliarity with the Constitution mentioned previously.

H. Unfamiliarity with Provincial Constitutions

162. Even more noticeable is the degree of unfamiliarity with the Provincial Constitutions, with 91% of people who know little (48%) or nothing (43%) about them and 2% who did not answer. A scant 7% claims to know them fairly well (6%) and very well (1%).

There is a sizeable difference between the indicators of zero or little knowledge in the City of Buenos Aires, in the metropolitan area and in Rosario, when compared with Córdoba, San Miguel de Tucumán or Mar del Plata. The former reveal far less familiarity with the Provincial Constitutions. For example, 48% of interviewees in Buenos Aires, 50% of those in Gran Buenos Aires and 60% of those in Rosario claim to have no knowledge, in sharp contrast with the 25% in Mar del Plata, 30% in Córdoba or 31% in Mendoza.

I. Unfamiliarity with the Municipal Charter of Córdoba

163. The poll conducted in the City of Córdoba (being the only one of the cities polled that has its own charter) also revealed a high degree of unfamiliarity with this law (86%) as the total of those who professed to know little (32%) or nothing (54%) about it, with another 8% who did not know or did not answer the question. Only a meagre 6% claimed to know it fairly well (3%) and very well (3%).

§4. CONCLUSIONS AND PROPOSALS[278]

I. Conclusions

164. The data from this enquiry produced good and bad news. On the positive side is the high appreciation that the majority of the people polled have of the Constitution and the fact that respect for the law appears as the most desired goal for the Argentine people. The enforcement of and respect for the laws are also seen as the most crucial factor for strengthening democracy, along with honest, transparent and accountable governments.

Yet the enquiry also revealed some brutally honest answers and disturbing news, including a poor knowledge of the Constitution and great disrespect for legality. Eighty-six per cent of the population polled thinks that Argentina lives most of the time on the wrong side of the law. Particularly serious is the fact that politicians primarily (74%), followed by the police (56%), public officials (49%) and judges (41%) are perceived to be the principal violators of the law. Another unpleasant surprise is that 88% of interviewees think Argentines are lawbreakers – even though the majority do not rate themselves as such.

In sum, a social and institutional order where neither citizens nor authorities obey and respect the law, and where the government neither imposes nor guarantees its

278. We follow in this topic our book Encuesta de Cultura Constitucional. Argentina: una sociedad anómica, Hernández, Zovatto and Mora y Araujo. *See* Hernández (2005).

enforcement, is the opinion that most Argentines have of this society. That perception extends to the National Constitution and speaks for the low level of trust in government institutions. It is the picture of an anomic society.

These data highlight the great paradox within Argentine society today: on the one hand, an enormous demand for legality, a high appraisal of the Constitution and a demand for leaders capable of obeying legislation, but on the other hand, a people who know little about their Constitution and obey it even less, who self-label themselves for the most part as transgressors and who, instead of assuming the responsibility for this transgression as their own, prefer to pass the buck to 'others'. This is a society in which 41% think there are times when it is necessary to disobey the law; 38% maintain that if they think they are right, they are willing to go against the law; and 23% are not willing to obey a decision they do not like, even if it has been made by the majority.

There is also a demand for equality, which is no small matter, inasmuch as the credibility of the institutions depends largely on that demand being met. In this sense, the poll brings to light another worrisome piece of information: the lack of trust in institutions, especially Congress and the political parties.

165. Particularly serious is the high level of mistrust of the Judiciary, which grows as we pass from lower judges to the national High Court of Justice. The judiciary is a cornerstone in any republican system. However, two decades after the birth of democracy, long delays by the judiciary, the difficulties to access it, the deterioration of its infrastructure, its lack of independence and suspicions of corruption hanging over some of its members have increased citizens' mistrust in this authority and, at the same time, stirred up a strong sensation of impunity.

We find the knowledge of institutional functions to be at an acceptable level, albeit not without a certain amount of confusion, especially regarding the functions of Congress and the nation's President, to the detriment of the former and benefit of the latter. That is a reflection of Argentine hyperpresidentialism, which has systematically upset the balance of powers provided for in the national Constitution, even during these two decades of democratic governments.

One of the most important assets achieved during the recent years of democratic life in Argentina is that the Argentine people value and support democracy. The data from the poll leave no doubt about that and are consistent with many other studies. At the same time, levels of discontent run high with regard to how well the democracy is working. Compared with the rest of Latin America, and according to data from the Latinobarometer, Argentina shows one of the highest support levels for democracy (73%) but, at the same time, little satisfaction with its performance. There is a large percentage of 'unsatisfied democrats' (34%), but that does not mean a majority in favour of military governments or other types of non-democratic systems.

Unfortunately, this support for democracy has not been accompanied by a progressive consolidation of a democratic republican regime and the rule of law. We have, on the contrary, been walking in the other direction. Democracy's chief attributes – citizens' control of government power, balance of powers, transparency and publicizing of government affairs – continue to be weak or non-existent.

Neither have we managed to galvanize the rule of law that is 'the subordination of all powers to the rule of law, from the lowest level to the very highest' (Norberto Bobbio). On the contrary, we can state, in light of the poll data, that there is a lack of consonance between laws and beliefs. The citizenry does not believe in the law-makers (members of Congress), in those who execute the laws (governors) or in those who interpret and enforce them (judiciary); and at times it does not establish precisely who is responsible for each one of those functions.

That is why it is imperative to bridge the gap that today separates society from its Constitution and its laws. But to do so, surmounting juridical and political obstacles alone is not enough. It is also necessary to make headway in a society's juridical culture, understood as, in the words of the Mexican constitutionalist Diego Valadés, 'the combination of ideas, convictions, perceptions, traditions and behaviours predominant in a community at a certain time in connection with the organization, functioning, effects and evolution of institutions'.

The Argentine people are aware that a minimal sense of responsibility exists with regard to the treatment of public property and spaces, basic rules for community living, mutual respect and beliefs about what is right and what is wrong. There is no sense of unity and responsibility among the population.

And there is no solid defence of freedom of the press, a *sine qua non* for any democratic and republican system, because although 53% are against the government controlling the press, a very high 40% are in favour.

Attitudes towards the death penalty, the detention of people without proof or vigilantism are equally disturbing inasmuch as they indicate conformity with more repressive positions that amount to a curb on individual rights and guarantees. These results should be analysed in the context of a society that admits to breaking the rules and having little respect for the law, a society that does not trust public institutions and perceives that the government and others do not obey the law.

On the subject of interpersonal trust, a key question for the generation of social capital, the Argentine people tend to place great trust in groups in their immediate environment (in the community in which they live) and very little in the institutions and social actors in organized society. At a local level (place of residence) six out of every ten Argentines (60%) say they have confidence in people. This degree of confidence and the perception of comradeship increase with the increased age, education and ranking on the social ladder; in contrast, the youngest members of the population are those who have the least confidence in others.

Regrettably, and as is the case in other countries, better schooling, a better income and belonging to younger age groups are not always factors that neutralize social practices or conceptions about legality that go against building a more tolerant, plural, open-society environment. On many topics, young people are the ones who show they know less and are less attached to or less respectful of the law or the Constitution.

166. This state of anomy calls for urgent reforms aimed at developing and firmly establishing in the Argentine society a true 'culture of legality'. However, we must be aware we cannot advance down the road of legal reforms without adequate observation of those reforms, because to do so would not only frustrate the population more but also risk weakening the already low levels of credibility and legitimacy of the main institutions.

We face, then, a deeply complex problem that has no simple answers in the short term. On the contrary, its solution requires a long-term comprehensive, ongoing strategy. It is a problem that cannot be solved by a ministry, or a body of inspectors, or a better-prepared, better-motivated police force or by any improvement of any partial aspect of the many that constitute this phenomenon.

We must realize that the responsibility is shared, and it is not only up to the governors, on whose shoulders obviously much of the responsibility falls, but also to the citizens. We must be frank enough and courageous enough to accept this diagnosis and admit that, as the poll confirms, we Argentines are habitual violators of the laws in force; we are very competent at fast discovering how to violate them and how to dodge punishment. We do not pay taxes as we should; we do not obey traffic regulations; we are always ready to slip a bribe; we look for exemptions of all kinds and have a very weak sense of community and so forth. From there, the anomic or illegal antics of Argentine society fan out into an astonishingly vast web.

We are a country known worldwide for admiring a goal scored with 'God's hand', for a Congress that applauds and celebrates the declaration of a default, for poor legal security, for the extreme danger in driving on our roads, for recurrent corruption scandals and high levels of impunity. It is not a question of exaggerating the significance of isolated deeds and symbols that can surely be explained in their context. But we shall not get very far if we do not admit that these deeds are manifestations of a recurrent pattern (a 'dumb' anomy, in the words of Carlos S. Nino), which clearly explains why we are a society with one of the lowest performances in the concert of nations. The anomy that burdens us is not only antidemocratic but it is also a leading cause of our underdevelopment.

Three angles can be used to tackle this problem: diagnosis, an analysis of the consequences and an analysis of what can be done. The diagnosis has been covered in the study presented here and begins to suggest the means for analysing the consequences and implications, and the formulation of proposals. Following is a preliminary list of some proposals that are intended more to suggest the idea of initiating a dialogue than to suggest a systematic approach. We will be more than satisfied if we can at least manage to promote public analysis and debate of this critical aspect of Argentine reality.

II. Proposals

167. It follows from everything analysed thus far that the priority is to achieve full enforcement of the National Constitution and the laws and to ensure that our republican institutions function properly, in accordance with the constitutional and democratic rule of law.

That implies full enforcement of citizens' rights, obligations and guarantees, and an adequate system of checks and balances of the authorities.

Without wishing to list too many items, we therefore recommend the following actions:

(1) Strengthen the activity of the National Congress and other legislative bodies in effectively performing their legislative duties and the political control of executive agencies. This means doing away with emergency legislation and the abusive practices of decrees of necessity and urgency and delegated legislation.
(2) Guarantee effective independence of the judges in the face of political authorities and other pressure or interest groups, and introduce a thorough amendment of judicial procedures.
(3) Promote in-depth civic and democratic education at every level of education. The great Austrian lawyer Hans Kelsen said that the first obligation of democracy was education for it. This implies revising study plans at different levels, both in the National Education Ministry and in the provinces and municipalities.
(4) Set up a commission in each chamber of Congress, as well as in the provincial legislatures and deliberating councils, to ensure an adequate tracking and control of compliance with laws passed.
(5) Ensure the right to access to information is effectively implemented, so as to have not only a more transparent government but also a more participative and better-informed society.
(6) Advance in political reform, in aspects connected with the electoral system, with the democratization, modernization and strengthening of the political parties, and with special focus on political financing. Promote the formation and training of political party leaders in interdisciplinary studies, including political science, constitutional law, public provincial law, municipal law, administrative law, Argentine history and constitutional history. There should be strict adherence to Article 38 of the National Constitution, which provides for the assignment of funds to political parties for this purpose.
(7) Ensure full enforcement of freedom of the press and freedom of expression. Ensure support from the media, public and private, so that they conduct a pedagogical campaign emphasizing the importance of the Constitution, the law and the institutions.
(8) Set up in the historic City of Santa Fe, which was the seat of our first Constitutional Congress, a national Constitution Centre for the conservation, diffusion and study of the Argentine Constitution. A noted example of such a move is the Centre of the United States Constitution recently inaugurated in Philadelphia.
(9) Demand knowledge of the Constitution in examinations for people competing for jobs in public office, as well as for awards to the Argentine people.
(10) Modify the study plans of law faculties to include the teaching of provincial public law and municipal law, because a greater in-depth knowledge of Provincial Constitutions and municipal charters is essential.

III. Brief Comment on the Second Survey on Constitutional Culture of 2014[279]

168. 'The weakness of the commitment of the Argentine society with its Constitution and laws, together with a serious deficit of institutional quality, lack of confidence and violence are the main conclusions that emerge from our second survey of constitutional culture, carried out together with Eduardo Fidanza, Director of Poliarquía, and that in general, confirm those observed 10 years ago, in the first survey, where we participated with Manuel Mora and Araujo.

Most of the interviewees perceive Argentina as an anomic society, in which laws in general and the Constitution in particular are not respected by citizens or by leaders.

The disaggregation of the data allows us to perceive the chiaroscuros of our society. In the positive terrain, the high valuation that the interviewees have of the Constitution and the fact that respect for the law appears as the most desired achievement for Argentines stand out. But the investigation also raises very worrying news, including a low degree of knowledge of the Constitution together with a high level of lack of respect for legality. 80% of the population interviewed considers that Argentina lives most of the time outside the law, while for 83% Argentines are disobedient and transgressors, although most do not locate themselves in that category. Particularly serious is the fact that politicians in the first place (with 74%), followed by police (52%), public officials (43%), people (39%) and judges (38%), are perceived as the biggest and main violators of the law.

Data show the abyss that exists between what we want to be as a society and what we are in reality: on the one hand, a high valuation of the Constitution (91% of the interviewed) and a demand for leaders capable of handling themselves in accordance with the laws, but, on the other, a society that knows and does not comply with its Constitution, since 73% recognizes it, with higher figures of ignorance of the Provincial Constitutions and Municipal Organic Letters: 87% and 94%, respectively, society that describes itself as a transgressor, and where 43% of the interviewed think there are times when it is necessary to disobey the law.

There is a strong demand for equality, since 63% believe that there is no equality before the law and 85% disagree with the phrase that Justice judges people regardless of their money.

The high distrust and the lack of credibility affect the main institutions, especially the Presidency, the Judiciary, the Congress, the unions and the political parties.

One of our strengths achieved in the last thirty-two years is that we Argentines value and support democracy. Unfortunately, this support for democracy has not been accompanied by a similar development in relation to the validity of the constitutional rule of Law. On the contrary, far from having progressively consolidated

279. Due to brevity reasons, we only present a brief comment on the Second Survey, following the Article 'La paradoja de nuestra sociedad' de Antonio María Hernández y Daniel Zovatto, in the Newspaper La Nación, Buenos Aires, 5 Apr. 2015. For further information, *see* Antonio María Hernández, Daniel Zovatto and Eduardo Fidanza Compiladores, Segunda Encuesta de Cultura Constitucional. Argentina: una sociedad anómica, before cited.

a republican and federal regime, we have walked in the opposite direction. Its main attributes – equality before the law, citizen control, responsibility of public officials, balance of powers, transparency and publicity of public affairs, federal principles and full autonomy of subnational governments – continue to be weak or absent. Special gravity assumes the inability of the State to prosecute drug trafficking, organized crime, corruption and the investigation of crimes that go unpunished, which increases distrust in institutions and especially in the Judiciary. Likewise, the violation of civil, political, economic, social and cultural rights of broad swaths of society cannot be ignored. To which is added a considerable increase in violence in all orders, which translates one of the most delicate problems in our history. There is a democracy with very low institutional quality and great weakness in its ethical, political, cultural and educational aspects' … . 'It is imperative to reverse the distance that separates society today from its Constitution and its laws through reforms aimed at developing and embedding in our society a "culture of legality". We are dealing with a complex, deep problem that does not have simple and specific answers. Its solution demands a comprehensive and long-term strategy. To advance in this process of change, we must start with the diagnosis: that of an anomie "stupid" and "antidemocratic", which is also one of the main causes of our underdevelopment (Nino). To which must be added the related problems of transgressions and violence, which require an emphasis on democratic education and, in particular, on a true pedagogy of the principles and values of the National Constitution, as established by another unfulfilled Law N° 25,863.'

Selected Bibliography

Alberdi, Juan Bautista. *Bases y puntos de partida para la organización política de la República Argentina.* Buenos Aires: Plus Ultra [1852] 1981.

Asociación Argentina de Derecho Constitucional. *A 10 años de la Reforma de la Constitución Nacional.* Córdoba: Advocatus, 2005.

Badeni, Gregorio. 'Constitucionalidad de la reforma constitucional'. *La Ley* 62, no. 143 (30 July 1998): 2.

Badeni, Gregorio. 'Límites de la delegación legislativa'. *La Ley.* 2001-E (2001): 1.

Bentham, Jeremy. *Tácticas Parlamentarias.* México: Ediciones Mesa Directiva, Senado de México, 2006.

Bianchi, Alberto. ' Los efectos del caso *Fayt* sobre la reforma constitucional de 1994'. *El Derecho.* Diario de Jurisprudencia y doctrina. (17 September 1999): 2.

Bianchi, Alberto. *El control de constitucionalidad.* 2nd edn. In two volumes. Buenos Aires: Editorial Abaco, 2002.

Bianchi, Alberto. 'La deuda institucional'. Revista del Colegio de Abogados de la ciudad de Buenos Aires. Tomo 67, no. 2 (December 2007): 42–55.

Bidart Campos, Germán. *Manual de Derecho Constitucional Argentino.* Buenos Aires: Ediar, 1972.

Bidart Campos, Germán. *El orden socioeconómico en la Constitución.* Buenos Aires: Ediar, 1999.

Bidart Campos, Germán. *Tratado Elemental del Derecho Constitucional Argentino.* t. I-A. Buenos Aires: Ediar, 2000a.

Bidart Campos, Germán. *Manual de la Constitución reformada.* t. II, 2da. reimpresión. Buenos Aires: Ediar, 2000b.

Bidart Campos, Germán. '¿Qué es una constitución?' *Revista Argentina de Derecho Constitucional* I, no. 1, Ediar (2000c): 3–17.

Botana, Natalio. *Poder y hegemonía.* Buenos Aires: Emecé Editores, 2007.

Colautti, Carlos E. 'Los derechos patrimoniales durante la emergencia'. *La Ley* t. 1991-E, 1359 y sgts, 1991.

Consejo Para La Consolidación De La Democracia. *Reforma Constitucional. Dictamen Preliminar.* Buenos Aires: Eudeba, 1986.

Demicheli, Alberto. *Formación nacional argentina.* Buenos Aires: Depalma, 1971.

Ekmekdjian, Miguel A. *Tratado de Derecho Constitucional.* Buenos Aires: Depalma, t. II, 1993.

Ekmekdjian, Miguel A. *Tratado de Derecho Constitucional.* Buenos Aires: Depalma, t. III, 1995.

Ekmekdjian, Miguel A. *Tratado de Derecho Constitucional.* Buenos Aires: Depalma, t. IV, 1997.

Fayt, Carlos S. *El self moving-Garantía de Independencia del Poder Judicial – La inamovilidad de los jueces federales, nacionales y provinciales.* Buenos Aires: La Ley, 2000.

Ferreira Rubio, Delia & Goretti Matteo. *Gobierno por decreto en Argentina. 1989–1993.* Buenos Aires: El Derecho. t. 1994. 158–748.

Frías, Pedro J. *Introducción al derecho público provincial.* Buenos Aires: Desalma, 1980.

Frías, Pedro J. *Derecho público provincial.* Buenos Aires: Desalma, 1985.

Garcia-Pelayo, Manuel. *Derecho Constitucional comparado.*6th edn. Madrid: Manuales de la Revista de Occidente, 1961.

Gargarella, Roberto. *La justicia frente al government.* Barcelona: Ariel, 1996.

Gelli, María Angélica. 'Controles sobre los decretos de necesidad y urgencia. De *Rodríguez* a *Verrochi.* El regreso de *Peralta*', *La Ley, Suplemento de Jurisprudencia de Derecho Administrativo.* Buenos Aires, La Ley, 14 February 2000.

Gelli, María Angélica. *Constitución de la Nación Argentina Comentada y Concordada*, Buenos Aires: La Ley, 2001.

González, Joaquín V. *Manual de la Constitución Argentina.* 1st edn. Buenos Aires: Angel Estrada y Cía. S.A., 1907.

Gordillo, Agustín, et al. *Derechos Humanos. Doctrina, casos y materiales. Parte General.* 2nd edn. Buenos Aires: Fundación de Derecho Administrativo, 1996.

Hamilton, A., J. Madison & J. Jay. *El Federalista.* México: Fondo de Cultura Económica, 2006.

Hernández, Antonio María. *Reforma constitucional de 1994. Labor del Convencional Constituyente Antonio María Hernández.* Buenos Aires: H. Cámara de Diputados de la Nación Argentina, 1995a.

Hernández, Antonio María. *Labor Parlamentaria, Dr. Antonio María Hernández (h.), Diputado de la Nación.* Buenos Aires: H. Cámara de Diputados de la Nación Argentina, 1995b.

Hernández, Antonio María. *Federalismo, autonomía municipal y ciudad de Buenos Aires en la reforma constitucional de 1994.* Buenos Aires: Depalma, 1997a.

Hernández, Antonio María. *Derecho Municipa.* T. 1, 2nd edn. Buenos Aires: Depalma, 1997b.

Hernández, Antonio María. *Integración y globalizacion: rol de las regiones, provincias y municipios.* Buenos Aires: Depalma, 2000.

Hernández, Antonio María. *El caso* Fayt *y sus implicancias constitucionales.* Córdoba: Academia Nacional de Derecho y Ciencias Sociales de Córdoba, 2001.

Hernández, Antonio María. 'La inconstitucionalidad del corralito financiero y bancario'. In *Revista de Derecho Público.* 2002-1. Buenos Aires: Rubinzal-Culzoni Editores, 2002.

Hernández, Antonio María. *Las emergencias y el orden constitucional.* 2nd edn. México: Instituto de Investigaciones Jurídicas de la Universidad Autónoma de México y Rubinzal-Culzoni Editores, 2003a.

Hernández, Antonio María. *Derecho Municipal. Parte General.* México, ed. Universidad Nacional Autónoma de Méjico, 2003b.

Hernández, Antonio. Las emergencias y la afectación del orden constitucional y de los derechos. In Hernández, A., Albanese, Susana, Alberto R. Dalla Via, Gargarella, Roberto y Sabsay, Daniel. *Derecho Constitucional*, Buenos Aires: Editorial Universidad, Prólogo de Giuseppe de Vergottini, 2004a, 319–407.

Hernández, Antonio María. *Federalismo y autonomía*. Editorial Ariel, España: Director Enric Argullol Murgadas, 2004b.

Hernández, Antonio María. 'El federalismo a diez años de la reforma constitucional de 1994'. In *A una década de la reforma constitucional 1994–2004*, coordinated by Germán J. Bidart Campos & Andrés Gil Domínguez. Buenos Aires: Ediar, 2004c.

Hernández, Antonio María, Daniel Zovatto & Manuel Mora y Araujo. *Encuesta de cultura constitucional. Argentina. una sociedad anómica*. México: Universidad Nacional Autónoma de México, Asociación Argentina de Derecho Constitucional e IDEA Internacional, 2005.

Hernández, Antonio María. 'Argentina, Subnational Constitutional Law'. *International Encyclopaedia of Laws*. Suppl. 66. The Hague: Kluwer Law International, Supplement 66, 2005a.

Hernández, Antonio María. *La descentralización del poder en el Estado contemporáneo*. Director, Asociación Argentina de Derecho Constitucional e Instituto Italiano de Cultura de Córdoba, 2005b.

Hernández, Antonio María. 'Valoración de la reforma constitucional de 1994 en su décimo aniversario'. In *A 10 años de la reforma constitucional*. Asocación Argentina de Derecho Constitucional. Córdoba: Advocatus (2005c): 49–69.

Hernández, Antonio María. 'La Corte Suprema, garante de la autonomía municipal'. *Revista Debates*, Buenos Aires: Asociación Argentina de Derecho Constitucional (2005d): 146–158.

Hernández, Antonio María. 'La influencia de la Constitución norteamericana en el federalismo argentino y de la Constitución Española de 1978 en el constitucionalismo provincial'. In *Derecho Federal*. Cap. 2. Directed by Walter F. Carnota. Buenos Aires: Grün Editora, 2005e.

Hernández, Antonio María. 'Legislative, Executive and Judicial Governance in Federal Countries'. In *Global Dialogue on Federalism Series, Volume 3*, edited by Katy Le Roy & Cheryl Saunders. Canada: McGill-Queens University Press, Chapter of Argentina, 2006a.

Hernández, Antonio María y José M. Belisle. 'Regulación jurídica de los partidos políticos en Argentina'. In *Regulación jurídica de los partidos políticos en América Latina*, coordinated by Daniel Zovatto. México: IDEA Internacional – Instituto de Investigaciones Jurídicas UNAM, 2006b, 191–242.

Hernández, Antonio María. 'El caso *Massa* y el regreso a la jurisprudencia convalidatoria de la emergencia económica'. *La Ley*, Suplemento especial '*La emergencia y el caso* Massa. Buenos Aires (February 2007): 70–79.

Hernández, Antonio María, et al. *Constitucionalismo en tiempos de emergencia*. con la coautoría de Alan Brewer Carías, Laurence Burgorgue-Larsen, José Luis Cea Egaña, Byung Yoon Cho, Alberto Dalla Via, David Dizenhaus, Lech Garlicki, Fortunato González Cruz, Michel Rosenfeld, Daniel Sabsay, Néstor Sagüés, Cheryl Saunders, Jorge Vanossi & el suscripto. Córdoba: Advocatus, 2007.

Selected Bibliography

Hernández, Antonio María (coord.). *Derecho Público Provincial*. Buenos Aires: Lexis Nexis, 2008a.

Hernández, Antonio María. 'Los derechos y deberes en nuestro constitucionalismo subnacional'. In *Derecho Público Provincial*, coordinated by Antonio M. Hernández. Buenos Aires: Lexis Nexis (2008b): 273–297.

Hernández, Antonio María. 'La Ciudad de Buenos Aires'. In *Derecho Público Provincial*, coordinated by Antonio M. Hernández. Buenos Aires: Lexis Nexis (2008c): 597–648.

Hernández, Antonio María. (2008d): 'Así no va más'-'Diagnóstico y propuestas de reforma político-electoral de la Provincia de Córdoba', de la Comisión Consultiva de Expertos que integrara, editado por las Universidades Nacional y Católica de Córdoba, Coautor.

Hernández, Antonio María. (2008e): 'Aspectos fiscales y económicos del federalismo argentino', Director y Coautor, Instituto de Federalismo de la Academia Nacional de Derecho y Ciencias Sociales de Córdoba, Córdoba.

Hernández, Antonio María. (2009a): 'Argentina, Constitutional Law', International Encyclopaedia of Laws, Kluwer Law International, Suppl. 81, (2009), Holanda, in English.

Hernández, Antonio María. (2009b): 'Federalismo y constitucionalismo provincial', Abeledo Perrot, Buenos Aires.

Hernández, Antonio María. (2009c): 'Aspectos históricos y políticos del federalismo argentino', Director y Coautor, Instituto de Federalismo de la Academia Nacional de Derecho y Ciencias Sociales de Córdoba, Córdoba

Hernández, Antonio María. (2011a): 'Argentina, Subnational Constitutional Law', International Encyclopaedia of Laws, Kluwer Law International, Suppl. 90, (2011), in English.

Hernández, Antonio María. (2011b): 'Derecho Público Provincial', 2ª. Edición, Coordinador y Coautor, Abeledo Perrot, Buenos Aires.

Hernández, Antonio María. (2012a): 'El caso "Fayt"', 2ª. Edición, Abeledo Perrot, Buenos Aires.

Hernández, Antonio María. (2012b): 'Derecho Constitucional', 2 Tomos, La Ley, Buenos Aires, 2012, Director y Coautor.

Hernández, Antonio María. (2012c): 'Fortalezas y Debilidades Constitucionales'-Una mirada crítica en el Bicentenario', Abeledo Perrot, Buenos Aires.

Hernández, Antonio María. (2012d): 'Cumplir el programa constitucional', IML, Buenos Aires, 2012.

Hernández, Antonio María, 'Constitutional Law in Argentina', International Encyclopaedia of Laws, Kluwer Law International, 2a. edition, Suppl. 110, (2014), in English.

Hernández Antonio María, 'El régimen municipal argentino', in 'Derecho Municipal Multinacional', Dirección de Teresita Rendón Huerta, Ed. Porrúa, Méjico, 2015.

Hernández Antonio María, Daniel Zovatto y Eduardo Fidanza, Compiladores, *'Segunda Encuesta de Cultura constitucional. Argentina: una sociedad anómica'*, Eudeba, Buenos Aires, 2016.

Hernández Antonio María, 'La Ciudad Autonóma de Buenos Aires y el fortalecimiento del federalismo argentino', Jusbaires, Buenos Aires, 2017.

Hesse, Honrad. *Escritos de derecho constitucional.* Madrid, Centro de Estudios Constitucionales, transl. Pedro Cruz Villalón, 1983.

Hutchinson, Tomás. 'La emergencia y el Estado de Derecho'. In *Revista de Derecho Público.* Buenos Aires: Rubinzal-Culzoni Editories, 2002.

Jaureguiberry, Luis María. *El Artículo Nuevo.* Santa Fe: Editorial Castellvi, 1957.

Lazzarini, José Luis. 'La emergencia en la doctrina de la Corte Suprema de la Nación'. *La Ley.* t. 1991-E, Secc. Doctrina, 1467 y sgts, 1991.

Levene, Ricardo. 'Los sucesos de Mayo'. In Volume V of *Historia de la Nación Argentina.* Segunda sección. 2nd edn. Director general Ricardo Levene. Buenos Aires: Librería y Editorial El Ateneo, 1941: 11–40.

Linares Quintana, Segundo V. *Tratado de la Ciencia del Derecho Constitucional Argentino y Comparado.* Tomo II, Buenos Aires: Alfa, 1953.

Luna, Félix. *Buenos Aires y el país.* 6th edn. Buenos Aires: Sudamericana, 1985.

Maljar, Daniel Edgardo. 'Antecedentes jurisprudenciales de la Corte Suprema sobre el derecho de emergencia. El principio de razonabilidad utilizado como limite'. *El Derecho, Suppl. D. Constitucional* (8 May 2002): 2.

Midón Mario R. *Decretos de Necesidad y Urgencia: En la Constitución Nacional y los ordenamientos provinciales.* Buenos Aires: La Ley, 2001.

Negretto, Gabriel L. 'Emergencia y crisis constitucional en la Argentina'. *El Derecho.* Tomo 154, 1989: 883.

Nino, Carlos Santiago. *Fundamentos de Derecho Constitucional.* Análisis filosófico, jurídico y politológico de la práctica constitucional. Buenos Aires: Astrea, 1992a.

Nino, Carlos Santiago. *Un país al margen de la ley.* 1st edn. Buenos Aires: Emecé, 1992b.

Nino, Carlos Santiago. *Un país al margen de la ley.* 3rd edn. Buenos Aires: Ariel, 2005.

Ortiz Pellegrini, Miguel Angel & Aguirre Susana Liliana. *Los Decretos de necesidad y urgencia en la Constitución Nacional de 1994.* Córdoba: Ed. Lerner, 1995.

Padilla, Miguel. 'El Congreso ha renunciado a sus atribuciones constitucionales'. *El Derecho.* Derecho Constitucional (18 February 2002): 5.

Palacio de Caeiro, Silvia B. 'Bases para el control de constitucionalidad de la legislacion delegante y delegada (artículo 76 de la Constitución Nacional)'. *La Ley* 2-XI (2001): 3–6.

Pérez Hualde, Alejandro. *Decretos de necesidad y urgencia.* Buenos Aires: Depalma, 1995.

Pérez Hualde, Alejandro. 'El Congreso Nacional Argentino frente a la crisis'. *El Derecho.* Derecho Constitucional (18 February 2002a): 16–17.

Pérez Hualde, Alejandro. 'Smith, o el final del sistema jurídico de la emergencia'. 'Depósitos bancarios Restricciones II'. Suplemento especial de la *Revista Jurídica Argentina La Ley* 8 (2002b).

Quiroga Lavié, Humberto. *El Poder Constituyente en acción.* Buenos Aires: Editorial Abaco, 1996.

Rébora, Juan Carlos. 'El 'estado' de asamblea'. *La Ley.* Páginas de Ayer, no. 10 (27 November 2001).

Romero, César Enrique. *El Poder Ejecutivo en la realidad política contemporánea.* España: Rev. De Estudios Polìticos de Madrid, 1963.

Sabsay, Daniel. 'Legislative Power'. In Susana Albanese, Alberto R. Dalla Via, Roberto Gargarella, Antonio M. Hernández and Daniel Sabsay *Derecho Constitucional (Constitutional Law).* Buenos Aires: Editorial Universidad, 2004a: 547–588.

Sabsay, Daniel. 'Poder Ejecutivo'. In Susana Albanese, Alberto R. Dalla Via, Roberto Gargarella, Antonio M. Hernández & Daniel Sabsay. *Derecho Constitucional (Constitutional Law).* Buenos Aires: Editorial Universidad, (2004b): 589–631.

Sagüés, Néstor Pedro. *Elementos de Derecho Constitucional.* Buenos Aires: Astrea, t. I y II, 1997.

Sagüés, Néstor Pedro. *La interpretación judicial de la Constitución.* Buenos Aires: Depalma, 1998.

Sagüés, Néstor Pedro. 'El derecho de amparo en Argentina'. In *El derecho de amparo en el mundo*, coordinated by Héctor Fix Zamudio & Eduardo Ferrer. Mexico: Mac-Gregor – Universidad Nacional Autónoma de Méjico – Porrúa and the Konrad Adenauer Stiftung, 2006.

Saguir, Julio. *Unión o Secesión?* Buenos Aires: Prometeo, 2007.

Spota (h.), Alberto. 'El control de constitucionalidad sobre las constituciones provinciales'. *La Ley* t. 2004-C-1090, 2004.

Tribe, Laurence H. *American Constitutional Law.*2nd edn. Mineola, NY: The Foundation Press, Inc., 1988.

Valadés, Diego. *El Gobierno de Gabinete.* México: Instituto de Investigaciones Jurídicas – UNAM, 2003.

Valadés, Diego. *La parlamentarización de los sistemas presidenciales.* México: Instituto de Investigaciones Jurídicas – UNAM – Colegio Nacional de México, 2007.

Vanossi, Jorge R. *El Estado de Derecho en el Constitucionalismo Social.* Buenos Aires: Eudeba, 1982.

Vanossi, Jorge R & Fermín Pedro Ubertone. 'Control jurisdiccional de constitucionalidad'. In *Desafíos del control de constitucionalidad*, coordinated by Víctor Bazán. Buenos Aires: Ediciones Ciudad Argentina 1996: 43–95.

Vanossi, Jorge R. *Teoría Constitucional.*2nd edn. Buenos Aires: Depalma, 2000.

Zarza Mensaque Alberto. *La region como alternative federal.* Boletíb de la Facultad de Derecho y Ciencias Sociales de la Universidad Nacional de Córdoba, 1977. no. 1 y 2, Córdoba.

Ziulu, Adolfo Gabino. *Estado de sitio: Emergencia necesaria o autoritarismo encubierto.* Buenos Aires: Depalma, 2000.

Zorraquín Becú, Ricardo. *El federalismo argentino.* Buenos Aires: Perrot, 1958.

Index

The numbers here refer to paragraph numbers.

Index

Made in the USA
Monee, IL
18 October 2026

66041410R10090